# THE YOUNG FOLKS'
# BOOK OF MIRTH

*A Collection of the Best Fun in
Prose and Verse*

# THE YOUNG FOLKS' BOOK OF MIRTH

A Collection of the Best Fun in
Prose and Verse

Selected by
MARY ROENAH THOMAS

*Granger Index Reprint Series*

BOOKS FOR LIBRARIES PRESS
FREEPORT, NEW YORK

First Published 1924
Reprinted 1972

INTERNATIONAL STANDARD BOOK NUMBER:
0-8369-6336-9


LIBRARY OF CONGRESS CATALOG CARD NUMBER:
75-38604


PRINTED IN THE UNITED STATES OF AMERICA
BY
NEW WORLD BOOK MANUFACTURING CO., INC.
HALLANDALE, FLORIDA 33009

*To all those who enjoy
innocent mirth*

# PREFACE

THE following sentence from Ruth's autobiography suggested the present volume:—" I was one year in Grade Seven and during that time our class never laughed once."

Although a possible exaggeration, it was this obvious regret that led the writer to consider whether in our educative process we are recognizing the value of the mind play which grows out of intellectual laughter, or whether by repression we are losing that quickness of insight and versatility which constitutes one of our mental assets.

The mission of this book is to call attention to the rightful place of laughter in life; to provide a proper field for the development of the fun-loving instinct present in every normal boy and girl, and to emphasize the fact that, with the same wise guidance and sympathetic censorship that is practised in other channels of development, the impulse to laugh at the coarse and vulgar will be replaced by a love for refined merriment.

Laughter is an escape from the serious attitude which the earnestness of life imposes upon us. The sense of humor which provokes laughter softens the discomforts, unfreezes coldness, and extends the youthful spirit into old age. With those who possess a fund of humor, petty annoyances are laughed away at their approach.

Certain kinds of laughter possess a social character. To substitute a joke for an argument tends to call the play mood into the minds of the disputants, the humor of the situation bringing instant relief; whereas, reason might have been slower and might have produced less happy results.

Since the quality of the laugh will always be a result of the moral view of the laughter, in cultivating a true sense of humor, we are indirectly teaching morals.

It is the business of our educators to cultivate a taste for humor by offering that form of good sentiment in the comic which will supplant the sort that is so deleterious, not only to the one who laughs but to the one laughed at.

A study of the lives of great men furnishes ample proof of the fact that a sense of humor is a feature of their minds. Of our three greatest Americans, Washington, Franklin, and Lincoln, the two latter were humorists. It was Lincoln's fund of humor that enabled him to see things in right proportion. " I never go snipe-shooting when bears are in sight," said he.    Even staid old Dr. Johnson writes:

> " If a man who turnips cries,
>   Cries not when his father dies,
>   'Tis a proof that he would rather
>   Have a turnip than his father."

Furthermore, if laughter is an escape from the serious attitude which the responsibilities of life impose upon us, it follows that we must keep this safety-valve under control, and the training of the impulse to laugh furnishes one of the best exercises for self-restraint and temperance.

There may be some persons who still believe that humor is synonymous with derision and flippancy, but these persons have not a correct idea of humor; for humor is seldom devoid of tenderness.    It is often the " one touch " needed to make the whole world kin.

Aside from the comic sheets of pictorial art, of modern caricature, and the stage, the greatest stimulus to the sense of humor is found in literature. Accordingly, this book has been prepared.    The selections herein contained are the result of a study of the best American and English writers of humor.

All varieties of humor are here represented, from the sweet merriment of James Whitcomb Riley to the more obvious and boisterous type of Edward

Lear. Even educationally considered, no hesitation is felt in using extracts from Joel Chandler Harris, from James Russell Lowell, and from others, for the reason that the spelling, although incorrect, reproduces a dialect and is therefore legitimate; and from Josh Billings and Artemus Ward because, though they do not give us a genuine Yankee dialect, they have the peculiar genius to make their letters " do the grinning for us."

Many of the selections are taken from writers of our own time in order that young readers may feel that humor is a living thing and that it has actual connection with everyday life. The extracts are of sufficient length to give a clear idea of the author's manner of fun-making, as well as to awaken a desire to read more of his works.

It is acknowledged that one of the safest guides to the study of one's disposition is an observation of that individual's laughter and the quality of his mirth. It will be found that in early childhood, only physical discomforts to somebody or to something appear ludicrous; but with intellectual growth comes an appreciation of mental tricks, and a sense of humor that is impersonal.

The present volume is therefore offered to all who enjoy pure mirth, and while it is a compilation of humor, it is presented to its readers with an earnest belief that their serious work will be taken up with a quicker pulse and with a more vigorous mind after an hour spent in the company of wholesome and nourishing fun.

MARY ROENAH THOMAS.

# CONTENTS

# 18    CONTENTS

# INDEX OF AUTHORS

# THE YOUNG FOLKS'
# BOOK OF MIRTH

# The Young Folks' Book of Mirth

## THE OWL AND THE PUSSY-CAT

### Edward Lear

The Owl and the Pussy-Cat went to sea
In a beautiful pea-green boat:
They took some honey, and plenty of money
Wrapped up in a five-pound note.
The Owl looked up to the stars above,
And sang to a small guitar,
"Oh, lovely Pussy, oh, Pussy, my love,
What a beautiful Pussy you are,
You are,
You are!
What a beautiful Pussy you are!"

Pussy said to the Owl, "You elegant fowl,
How charmingly sweet you sing!
Oh, let us be married; too long we have tarried:
But what shall we do for a ring?"

They sailed away for a year and a day
　　To the land where the bong-tree grows;
And there in the wood a Piggy-wig stood,
　　With a ring at the end of his nose,
　　　　His nose,
　　　　His nose,
With a ring at the end of his nose.

"Dear Pig, are you willing to sell for one
　　　shilling
　　Your ring?"　Said the Piggy, " I will."
So they took it away and were married next
　　　day
　　By the Turkey who lives on the hill.
They dined upon mince and slices of quince,
　　Which they ate with a runcible spoon;
And hand in hand, on the edge of the sand,
　　They danced by the light of the moon,
　　　　The moon,
　　　　The moon,
They danced by the light of the moon.

# LAUGHING

## Henry W. Shaw
### (Josh Billings)

It never haz been proved, that enny ov the animal kreation hav attempted tew laff, (we are quite certain that none hav succeeded;) thus this deliteful episode and pleasant power appears tew be entirely within the province ov humans.

It iz the language ov infancy—the eloquence ov childhood,—and the power tew laff is the power to be happy.

It iz becoming tew awl ages and conditions; and (with the very few exceptions, sakred tew sorrow) an honest, hearty laff iz always agreeable and in order.

It iz an index ov karakter, and betrays sooner than words.

Laffing keeps oph sickness, and haz conquered az menny diseases az ever pills have, and at mutch less expense.—It makes flesh, and keeps it in its place. It drives away weariness and brings a dream ov sweetness tew the sleeper.—It never iz covetous.— It ackompanys charity, and iz the handmaid ov honesty.—It disarms revenge, humbles pride, and iz the talisman ov kontentment.—Sum have kalled it a weekness—a substitute for thought, but really it strengthens wit, and adorns wisdum, invigorates the mind, gives language ease, and expreshen elegance. —It holds the mirror up tew beauty: it strengthens modesty, and makes virtew heavenly.

It iz the light ov life; without it we should be but animated ghosts.

It challenges fear, hides sorrow, weakens despair, and carries haff ov poverty's bundles.—It costs nothing, comes at the call, and leaves a brite spot behind.—It iz the only index ov gladness, and the only buty that time kannot effase.—It never grows old: it reaches from the cradle clear to the grave.

Without it, love would be no pashun, and fruition would show no joy.—It iz the fust and the last sunshine that visits the heart.

A Good Rezolushun:

That i will laff every good chance i kan git, whether it makes me gro phatt or not.

Josh Billings.

# GOOD COUNSEL

CAROLYN WELLS

LITTLE children, always be
Kind to everything you see.
Do not kick the table's legs,
Don't beat unoffending eggs.

Do not mischievously try
To poke things in a needle's eye;
Nor guilty be of such a fault
As to pinch the table salt.

Do not pull a teapot's nose,
Don't ask bread what time it rose.
Little pitchers' ears don't tweak,
Nor smack the apple's rosy cheek.

But remember it is right
To all things to be polite;
Let the hay-scales have their weigh,
Wish the calendar good day.

Kiss the clock upon its face,
Return the armchair's fond embrace,
Greet the sieve in merry strain,
Ask the window how's its pane.

If you learn to show such traits
To your dumb inanimates,
Toward your playmates then you'll find
You've an amiable mind.

# A PETITION OF THE LEFT HAND

## Benjamin Franklin

I ADDRESS myself to all the friends of youth, and conjure them to direct their compassionate regards to my unhappy fate, in order to remove the prejudices of which I am the victim. There are twin sisters of us; and the two eyes of man do not more resemble, nor are capable of being upon better terms with each other, than my sister and myself, were it not for the partiality of our parents, who make the most injurious distinctions between us. From my infancy, I have been led to consider my sister as a being of a more elevated rank. I was suffered to grow up without the least instruction, while nothing was spared in her education. She had masters to teach her writing, drawing, music, and other accomplishments; but if by chance I touched a pencil, a pen, or a needle, I was bitterly rebuked; and more than once I have been beaten for being awkward, and wanting a graceful manner. It is true, my sister associated me with her upon some occasions; but she always made a point of taking the lead, calling upon me only from necessity, or to figure by her side.

But conceive not, Sirs, that my complaints are instigated merely by vanity. No; my uneasiness is occasioned by an object much more serious. It is the practice in our family, that the whole business of providing for its subsistence falls upon my sister and myself. If any indisposition should attack my sister,—and I mention it in confidence upon this occasion that she is subject to the gout, rheumatism, and cramp, without making mention of other accidents,—what would be the fate of our poor family? Must not the regret of our parents be excessive, at having placed so great a difference between sisters who are so perfectly equal? Alas! we must perish from distress; for it would not be in my power even to scrawl a suppliant petition for relief, having been obliged to employ the hand of another in transcribing the request which I have now the honor to prefer to you.

Condescend, Sirs, to make my parents sensible of the injustice of an exclusive tenderness, and of the necessity of distributing their care and affection among all their children equally. I am, with a profound respect, Sirs, your obedient servant,

THE LEFT HAND.

# NO!

## Thomas Hood

No sun—no moon!
  No morn—no noon—
No dawn—no dusk—no proper time of day—
  No sky—no earthly view—
  No distance looking blue—
No road—no street—no " t'other side the
      way "—
  No end to any Row—
  No indications where the Crescents go—
  No top to any steeple—
No recognitions of familiar people—
  No courtesies for showing 'em—
  No knowing 'em!
No traveling at all—no locomotion,
No inkling of the way—no notion—
" No go "—by land or ocean—
  No mail—no post—
  No news from any foreign coast—
No park—no ring—no afternoon gentility—
  No company—no nobility—

No warmth, no cheerfulness, no healthful ease,
No comfortable feel in any member—
No shade, no shine, no butterflies, no bees,
No fruits, no flowers, no leaves, no birds,
November.

# THE EMPEROR'S NEW CLOTHES

## Hans Christian Andersen

Many years ago there was an emperor who was so excessively fond of new clothes that he spent all his money on them. He cared nothing about his soldiers nor for the theatre, nor for driving in the woods except for the sake of showing off his new clothes. He had a costume for every hour in the day, and instead of saying as one does about any other king or emperor, " He is in his council chamber," here one always said, " The emperor is in his dressing-room."

Life was very gay in the great town where he lived; hosts of strangers came to visit it every day, and among them one day two swindlers. They gave themselves out as weavers, and said that they knew how to weave the most beautiful stuffs imaginable. Not only were the colors and patterns unusually fine, but the clothes that were made of the stuffs had the peculiar quality of becoming invisible to every person who was not fit for the office he held, or if he was impossibly dull.

" These must be splendid clothes," thought the emperor. " By wearing them I should be able to discover which men in my kingdom are unfitted for their posts. I shall distinguish the wise men from the fools. Yes, I certainly must order some of that stuff to be woven for me."

He paid the two swindlers a lot of money in advance so that they might begin their work at once.

They did put up two looms and pretended to weave, but they had nothing whatever upon their shuttles. At the outset they asked for a quantity of the finest silk and the purest gold thread, all of which they put into their own bags while they worked away at the empty looms far into the night.

"I should like to know how those weavers are getting on with the stuff," thought the emperor; but he felt a little queer when he reflected that any one who was stupid or unfit for his post would not be able to see it. He certainly thought that he need have no fears for himself, but still he thought he would send somebody else first to see how it was getting on. Everybody in the town knew what wonderful power the stuff possessed, and every one was anxious to see how stupid his neighbor was.

"I will send my faithful old minister to the weavers," thought the emperor. "He will be best able to see how the stuff looks, for he is a clever man and no one fulfills his duties better than he does!"

So the good old minister went into the room

where the two swindlers sat working at the empty loom.

"Heaven preserve us!" thought the old minister, opening his eyes very wide. "Why, I can't see a thing!" But he took care not to say so.

Both the swindlers begged him to be good enough to step a little nearer, and asked if he did not think it a good pattern and beautiful coloring. They pointed to the empty loom, and the poor old minister stared as hard as he could, but he could not see anything, for of course there was nothing to see.

"Good heavens!" thought he, "is it possible that I am a fool? I have never thought so and nobody must know it. Am I not fit for my post? It will never do to say that I cannot see the stuffs."

"Well, sir, you don't say anything about the stuff," said the one who was pretending to weave.

"Oh, it is beautiful! quite charming!" said the old minister, looking through his spectacles; "this pattern and these colors! I will certainly tell the emperor that the stuff pleases me very much."

"We are delighted to hear you say so," said the swindlers, and then they named all the colors and described the peculiar pattern. The old minister paid great attention to what they said, so as to be able to repeat it when he got home to the emperor.

Then the swindlers went on to demand more money, more silk, and more gold, to be able to proceed with the weaving; but they put it all into their own pockets—not a single strand was ever put into the loom, but they went on as before, weaving at the empty loom.

The emperor soon sent another faithful official to see how the stuff was getting on, and if it would soon be ready. The same thing happened to him as to the minister; he looked and looked, but as there was only the empty loom, he could see nothing at all.

" Is not this a beautiful piece of stuff? " said both the swindlers, showing and explaining the beautiful pattern and colors which were not there to be seen.

" I know I am not a fool," thought the man, " so it must be that I am unfit for my good post. It is very strange, though; however, one must not let it appear." So he praised the stuff he did not see, and assured them of his delight in the beautiful colors and the originality of the design. " It is absolutely charming! " he said to the emperor. Everybody in the town was talking about this splendid stuff.

Now the emperor thought he would like to see it while it was still on the loom. So, accompanied by a number of selected courtiers, among whom were the two faithful officials who had already seen the imaginary stuff, he went to visit the crafty imposters, who were working away as hard as ever they could at the empty loom.

" It is magnificent!" said both the honest officials. " Only see, your Majesty, what a design! What colors!" And they pointed to the empty loom, for they thought no doubt the others could see the stuff.

" What!" thought the emperor; " I see nothing at all! This is terrible! Am I a fool? Am I not fit to be emperor? Why, nothing worse could happen to me!"

" Oh, it is beautiful!" said the emperor. " It has my highest approval!" and he nodded his satisfaction as he gazed at the empty loom. Nothing would induce him to say that he could not see anything.

The whole suite gazed and gazed, but saw nothing more than all the others. However, they all exclaimed with his Majesty, " It is very beautiful!" and they advised him to wear a suit of this wonderful cloth on the occasion of a great procession which was just about to take place. " It is magnificent! gorgeous! excellent!" went from mouth to mouth; they were all equally delighted with it. The em-

peror gave each of the rogues an order of knighthood to be worn in their buttonholes and the title
of " Gentlemen weavers."

The swindlers sat up the whole night, before the
day on which the procession was to take place, burning sixteen candles, so that people might see how
anxious they were to get the emperor's new clothes
ready.   They pretended to take the stuff off the
loom.   They cut it out in the air with a huge pair
of scissors, and they stitched away with needles
without any thread in them.   At last they said:
" Now the emperor's new clothes are ready!"

The emperor, with his grandest courtiers, went
to them himself, and both the swindlers raised one
arm in the air, as if they were holding something,
and said, " See, these are the trousers, this is the
coat, here is the mantle!" and so on.   " It is as
light as a spider's web.   One might think one had
nothing on, but that is the very beauty of it!"

" Yes!" said all the courtiers, but they could not
see anything, for there was nothing to see.

" Will your imperial Majesty be graciously
pleased to take off your clothes," said the imposters, " so that we may put on the new ones, along
here before the great mirror?"

The emperor took off all his clothes, and the imposters pretended to give him one article of dress

after the other, of the new ones which they had pretended to make. They pretended to fasten something round his waist and to tie on something; this was the train, and the emperor turned round and round in front of the mirror.

" How well his Majesty looks in the new clothes! How becoming they are!" cried all the people round. "What a design and what colors! They are most gorgeous robes!"

" The canopy is waiting outside which is to be carried over his Majesty in the procession," said the master of the ceremonies.

"Well, I am quite ready," said the emperor. "Don't the clothes fit well?" and then he turned round again in front of the mirror, so that he should seem to be looking at his grand things.

The chamberlains who were to carry the train stooped and pretended to lift it from the ground with both hands, and they walked along with their hands in the air. They dared not let it appear that they could not see anything.

Then the emperor walked along in the procession under the gorgeous canopy, and everybody in the streets and at the windows exclaimed, "How beautiful the emperor's new clothes are! What a splendid train! And they fit to perfection!" Nobody would let it appear that he could see nothing, for then he would not be fit for his post, or else he was a fool.

None of the emperor's clothes had been so successful before.

" But he has nothing on," said a little child.

" Oh, listen to the innocent," said its father; and one person whispered to the other what the child had said. " He has nothing on; a child says he has nothing on! "

" But he has nothing on! " at last cried all the people.

The emperor writhed, for he knew it was true, but he thought, " The procession must go on now," so he held himself stiffer than ever, and the chamberlains held up the invisible train.

# THE PURPLE COW

## Gelett Burgess

I never saw a Purple Cow,
  I never hope to see one;
But I can tell you, anyhow,
  I'd rather see than be one.

# THE CATARACT OF LODORE

Robert Southey

## 1

" How does the water
 Come down at Lodore? "
My little boy asked me
Thus, once on a time:
And moreover he tasked me
 To tell him in rhyme.
  Anon at the word,
There first came one daughter,
And then came another,
 To second and third
The request of their brother,
And to hear how the water
 Comes down at Lodore,
 With its rush and its roar,
  As many a time
They had seen it before.
 So I told them in rhyme,
For of rhymes I had store;
And 'twas in my vocation
 For their recreation

That so I should sing;
Because I was Laureate
  To them and the King.

2

From its sources which well
  In the tarn on the fell;
    From its fountains
    In the mountains,
  Its rills and its gills;
Through moss and through brake,
    It runs and it creeps
  For a while till it sleeps
    In its own little lake.
  And thence at departing,
  Awakening and starting,
It runs through the reeds,
  And away it proceeds,
Through meadow and glade,
  In sun and in shade,
And through the wood-shelter,
  Among crags in its flurry,
    Helter-skelter,
    Hurry-skurry,
  Here it comes sparkling,
  And there it lies darkling;
Now smoking and frothing

Its tumult and wrath in,
Till, in this rapid race
On which it is bent,
It reaches the place
Of its steep descent.

### 3

The cataract strong
Then plunges along,
Striking and raging,
As if a war waging
Its caverns and rocks among;
Rising and leaping,
Sinking and creeping,
Swelling and sweeping,
Showering and springing,
Flying and flinging,
Writhing and ringing,
Eddying and whisking,
Spouting and frisking,
Turning and twisting,
Around and around
With endless rebound!
Smiting and fighting,
A sight to delight in;
Confounding, astounding,
Dizzying and deafening the ear
with its sound.

4

Collecting, projecting,
Receding and speeding,
And shocking and rocking,
And darting and parting,
And threading and spreading,
And whizzing and hissing,
And dripping and skipping,
And hitting and spitting,
And shining and twining,
And rattling and battling,
And shaking and quaking,
And pouring and roaring,
And waving and raving,
And tossing and crossing,
And flowing and going,
And running and stunning,
And foaming and roaming,
And dinning and spinning,
And dropping and hopping,
And working and jerking,
And guggling and struggling,
And heaving and cleaving,
And moaning and groaning;


5

And glittering and frittering,

And gathering and feathering,
And whitening and brightening,
And quivering and shivering,
And hurrying and skurrying,
And thundering and floundering;
Dividing and gliding and sliding,
And falling and brawling and sprawling,
And driving and riving and striving,
And sprinkling and twinkling and wrinkling,
And sounding and bounding and rounding,
And bubbling and troubling and doubling,
And grumbling and rumbling and tumbling,
And clattering and battering and shattering;

## 6

Retreating and beating and meeting and sheeting,
Delaying and straying and playing and spraying,
Advancing and prancing and glancing and dancing,
Recoiling, turmoiling and toiling and boiling,
And gleaming and streaming and steaming and beaming,
And rushing and flushing and brushing and gushing,
And flapping and rapping and clapping and slapping,
And curling and whirling and purling and twirling,

And thumping and plumping and bumping and
    jumping,
And dashing and flashing and splashing and clash-
    ing;
And so never ending, but always descending,
Sounds and motions forever and ever are blend-
    ing,
All at once and all o'er, with a mighty uproar;
And this way the water comes down at Lodore.

# LITTLE BILLEE

## William Makepeace Thackeray

There were three sailors of Bristol City
    Who took a boat and went to sea,
But first with beef and captain's biscuits,
    And pickled pork they loaded she.

There was gorging Jack, and guzzling Jimmy,
    And the youngest he was little Billee.
Now when they'd got as far as the Equator,
    They'd nothing left but one split pea.

Says gorging Jack to guzzling Jimmy,
    " I am extremely hungaree."
To gorging Jack says guzzling Jimmy,
    " We've nothing left, us must eat we."

Says gorging Jack to guzzling Jimmy,
    " With one another we shouldn't agree!
There's little Bill, he's young and tender,
    We're old and tough, so let's eat he."

" O Billy! we're going to kill and eat you,
    So undo the button of your chemie."
When Bill received this information,
    He used his pocket-handkerchie.

" First let me say my catechism,
    Which my poor mother taught to me."
" Make haste! make haste! " says guzzling
        Jimmy,
    While Jack pulled out his snicker-snee.

Then Bill went up to the main-top-gallant-
        mast,
    And down he fell on his bended knee,
He scarce had come to the twelfth Com-
        mandment,
    When up he jumps—" There's land I see! "

" Jerusalem and Madagascar,
    And North and South Amerikee,
There's the British flag a-riding at anchor,
    With Admiral Napier, K. C. B."

So when they got aboard of the Admiral's,
    He hanged fat Jack and flogged Jimmee,
But as for little Bill, he made him
    The captain of a Seventy-three.

# THE GOLDEN REIGN OF WOUTER VAN TWILLER

## Washington Irving

It was in the year of our Lord 1629 that Mynheer Wouter Van Twiller was appointed governor of the province of Niew Nederlands, under the commission and control of their High Mightinesses the Lords States General of the United Netherlands, and the privileged West India Company.

This renowned old gentleman arrived at New Amsterdam in the merry month of June, the sweetest month in all the year; when Dan Apollo seems to dance up the transparent firmament—when the robin, the thrush, and a thousand other wanton songsters make the woods to resound with amorous ditties, and the luxurious little boblincon revels among the clover blossoms of the meadows—all which happy coincidence persuaded the old dames of New Amsterdam, who were skilled in the art of foretelling events, that this was to be a happy and prosperous administration.

The renowned Wouter (or Walter) Van Twiller was descended from a long line of Dutch burgo-

masters, who had successively dozed away their
lives, and grown fat upon the bench of magistracy
in Rotterdam; and who had comported themselves
with such singular wisdom and propriety, that they
were never either heard or talked of—which, next
to being universally applauded, should be the object of ambition of all magistrates and rulers.
There are two opposite ways by which some men
make a figure in the world; one by talking faster
than they think; and the other by holding their
tongues and not thinking at all.  By the first many
a smatterer acquires the reputation of a man of
quick parts; by the other many a dunderpate, like
the owl, the stupidest of birds, comes to be considered the very type of wisdom.  This, by the way,
is a casual remark, which I would not for the uni-
verse have it thought I apply to Governor Van
Twiller.  It is true he was a man shut up within
himself, like an oyster, and rarely spoke except in
monosyllables; but then it was allowed he seldom
said a foolish thing.  So invincible was his gravity
that he was never known to laugh or even smile
through the whole course of a long and prosperous
life.  Nay, if a joke were uttered in his presence,
that set light-minded hearers in a roar, it was observed to throw him into a state of perplexity.
Sometimes he would deign to inquire into the mat-

ter, and when, after much explanation, the joke was made as plain as a pikestaff, he would continue to smoke his pipe in silence, and at length, knocking out the ashes would exclaim, " Well! I see nothing in all that to laugh about."

With all his reflective habits, he never made up his mind on a subject. His adherents accounted for this by the astonishing magnitude of his ideas. He conceived every subject on so grand a scale that he had not room in his head to turn it over and examine both sides of it. Certain it is that if any matter ·were propounded to him on which ordinary mortals would rashly determine at first glance, he would put on a vague, mysterious look; shake his capacious head; smoke some time in profound silence, and at length observe that " he had his doubts about the matter," which gained him the reputation of a man slow of belief, and not easily imposed upon. What is more, it gained him a lasting name: for to this habit of the mind has been attributed his surname of Twiller; which is said to be a corruption of the original Twijfler, or in plain English, Doubter.

The person of this illustrious old gentleman was formed and proportioned, as though it had been moulded by the hands of some cunning Dutch statuary, as a model of majesty and lordly gran-

deur.  He was exactly five feet six inches in height,
and six feet five inches in circumference.  His head
was a perfect sphere, and of such stupendous di-
mensions, that dame Nature with all her sex's ingenuity, would have been puzzled to construct a
neck capable of supporting it; wherefore she wisely
declined the attempt, and settled it firmly on the
top of his backbone, just between the shoulders.
His body was oblong and particularly capacious at
bottom; which was wisely ordered by Providence,
seeing that he was a man of sedentary habits, and
very averse to the idle labor of walking.  His legs
were short, but sturdy in proportion to the weight
they had to sustain; so that when erect he had not
a little the appearance of a beer barrel on skids.  His
face, that infallible index of the mind, presented a
vast expanse, unfurrowed by any of those lines and
angles which disfigure the human countenance with
what is termed expression.  Two small gray eyes
twinkled feebly in the midst, like two stars of lesser
magnitude in a hazy firmament; and his full-fed
cheeks, which seemed to have taken toll of everything that went into his mouth, were curiously mot-
tled and streaked with dusky red, like a spitzenberg
apple.

His habits were as regular as his person.  He
daily took his four stated meals, appropriating ex-

actly an hour to each: he smoked and doubted eight hours, and he slept the remaining twelve of the four-and-twenty. Such was the renowned Wouter Van Twiller—a true philosopher, for his mind was either elevated above, or tranquilly settled below, the cares and perplexities of this world. He had lived in it for years, without feeling the least curiosity to know whether the sun revolved round it, or it round the sun: and he had watched, for at least half a century, the smoke curling from his pipe to the ceiling, without once troubling his head with any of those numerous theories by which a philosopher would have perplexed his brain, in accounting for its rising above the surrounding atmosphere.

.    .    .    .    .    .    .    .

I have been the more anxious to delineate fully the person and habits of Wouter Van Twiller, from the consideration that he was not only the first, but also the best governor that ever presided over this ancient and respectable province: and so tranquil and benevolent was his reign, that I do not find throughout the whole of it, a single instance of any offender being brought to punishment—a most indubitable sign of a merciful governor, and a case unparalleled, excepting in the reign of the illustrious King Log, from whom, it is hinted, the renowned Van Twiller was a lineal descendant.

The very outset of the career of this excellent magistrate was distinguished by an example of legal acumen, that gave flattering presage of a wise and equitable administration. The morning after he had been installed in office, and at the moment that he was making his breakfast from a prodigious earthen dish, filled with milk and Indian pudding, he was interrupted by the appearance of Wandle Schoonhoven, a very important old burgher of New Amsterdam, who complained bitterly of one Barent Bleecker, inasmuch as he refused to come to a settlement of accounts, seeing that there was a heavy balance in favor of the said Wandle. Governor Van Twiller, as I have already observed, was a man of few words: he was likewise a mortal enemy to multiplying writings—or being disturbed at his breakfast. Having listened attentively to the statement of Wandle Schoonhoven, giving an occasional grunt, as he shovelled a spoonful of Indian pudding into his mouth—either as a sign that he relished the dish, or comprehended the story—he called unto him his constable and pulling out of his breeches pocket a huge jack-knife, despatched it after the defendant as a summons, accompanied by his tobacco-box as a warrant.

This summary process was as effectual in those simple days as was the seal ring of the great

Haroun-al-Raschid among the true believers. The two parties being confronted before him, each produced a book of accounts, written in a language and character that would have puzzled any but a High Dutch commentator, or a learned decipherer of Egyptian obelisks.

The sage Wouter took them one after the other, and having poised them in his hands, and attentively counted over the number of leaves, fell straightway into a very great doubt, and smoked for half an hour without saying a word: at length, laying his finger beside his nose, and shutting his eyes for a moment, with the air of a man who has just caught a subtle idea by the tail, he slowly took his pipe from his mouth, puffed forth a column of tobacco smoke, and with marvellous gravity and solemnity, pronounced—that having carefully counted over the leaves and weighed the books, it was found, that one was just as thick and as heavy as the other—therefore it was the final opinion of the court that the accounts were equally balanced—therefore Wandle should give Barent a receipt, and Barent should give Wandle a receipt—and the constable should pay the costs.

This decision being straightway made known, diffused general joy throughout New Amsterdam, for the people immediately perceived that they had a very wise and equitable magistrate to rule over them. But its happiest effect was, that not another lawsuit took place throughout the whole of his administration—and the office of constable fell into such decay, that there was not one of those losel scouts known in the province for many years. I am the more particular in dwelling on this transaction, not only because I deem it one of the most sage and righteous judgments on record, and well worthy the attention of modern magistrates: but because it was a miraculous event in the history of the renowned Wouter—being the only time he was ever known to come to a decision in the whole course of his life.

# A CHRISTMAS EVE MONOLOGUE

### Frederick Moxon

*Time:* Ten o'clock. *Place:* Bed. *Speaker:* Ted.

" I JUST *wonder* if it's so?
Bob an' Jim had oughter know,
'Cause they both are older'n me;
Bob is nearly 'leven, an' he
Says he knows for *sure* an' Jim
Says his Pa owned up to him.   (*Yawns.*)

" An' I guess it's maybe right,
So I'm goin' to watch to-night.   (*Blinks and
  yawns.*)
I'll let on  .  .  .  to be asleep,
Then  .  .  .  I'll take a teeny peep.  .  .  .
Bob says  .  .  .  that our Mas an' Pas
Is the only  .  .  .  (*Yawns.*)  .  .  .  Santy
  Claus.   (*Blink, blink.*)

" I'll just  .  .  .  watch them fill  .  .  .  the
  socks,
Same as Jim did with his folks  .  .  .  (*Pause.*)
Then I'll see them  .  .  .  sneak away
To the door  .  .  .  (*Blink, blink.*) an' then
  I'll say,

' Oh, you *Santy Claus* ' . . . (*Deep sigh.*)

    . . . an' then—

. . . (*Silence.*) . . .

Gee! It's Christmas! *An' he's been!* "

> (*From " Judge," December 11, 1915.*)

# THE OWL-CRITIC

## James Thomas Fields

" Who stuffed that white owl? "   No one spoke
    in the shop,
  The barber was busy, and he couldn't stop;
  The customers, waiting their turns, were all read-
    ing
  The *Daily,* the *Herald,* the *Post,* little heeding
  The young man who blurted out such a blunt
    question;
Not one raised a head, or even made a sugges-
    tion;
      And the barber kept on shaving.

" Don't you see, Mr. Brown,"
  Cried the youth, with a frown,
" How wrong the whole thing is,
  How preposterous each wing is,
  How flattened the head is, how jammed down the
    neck is—
  In short, the whole owl, what an ignorant wreck
    'tis!
  I make no apology;
  I've learned owl-eology.

I've passed days and nights in a hundred collec-
    tions,
And cannot be blinded to any deflections
Arising from unskilful fingers that fail
To stuff a bird right, from his beak to his tail.
Mister Brown! Mister Brown!
Do take that bird down,
Or you'll soon be the laughing-stock all over
    town!"
      And the barber kept on shaving.

" I've *studied* owls,
  And other night fowls,
  And I tell you
  What I know to be true;
  An owl cannot roost
  With his limbs so unloosed;
  No owl in this world
  Ever had his claws curled,
  Ever had his legs slanted,
  Ever had his bill canted,
  Ever had his neck screwed
  Into that attitude.
  He can't *do* it, because
  'Tis against all bird laws.
  Anatomy teaches,
  Ornithology preaches

An owl has a toe
That can't turn out so!
I've made the white owl my study for years,
And to see such a job almost moves me to tears!
Mister Brown, I'm amazed
You should be so gone crazed
As to put up a bird
In that posture absurd!
To *look* at that owl really brings on a dizziness;
The man who stuffed *him* don't half know his
     business!' "
       And the barber kept on shaving.

" Examine those eyes.
I'm filled with surprise
Taxidermists should pass
Off on you such poor glass;
So unnatural they seem
They'd make Audubon scream,
And John Burroughs laugh
To encounter such chaff.
Do take that bird down;
Have him stuffed again, Brown!' "
       And the barber kept on shaving.

" With some sawdust and bark
I could stuff in the dark

An owl better than that.
I could make an old hat
Look more like an owl
Than that horrid fowl,
Stuck up there so stiff like a side of coarse
  leather.
In fact, about *him* there's not one natural
  feather."

Just then, with a wink and a sly normal lurch,
The owl, very gravely, got down from his perch,
Walked around, and regarded his fault-finding
  critic,
(Who thought he was stuffed) with a glance
  analytic,
And then fairly hooted, as if he should say:
" Your learning's at fault *this* time, anyway;
Don't waste it again on a live bird, I pray.
I'm an owl; you're another. Sir Critic, good
  day!"
    And the barber kept on shaving.

# GUIDO THE GIMLET OF GHENT: A ROMANCE OF CHIVALRY

## Stephen B. Leacock

It was in the flood-tide of chivalry. Knighthood was in the pod.

The sun was slowly setting in the east, rising and falling occasionally as it subsided, and illuminating with its dying beams the towers of the grim castle of Buggensberg.

Isolde the Slender stood upon an embattled turret of the castle. Her arms were outstretched to the empty air, and her face, upturned as if in colloquy with heaven, was distraught with yearning.

Anon she murmured, " Guido "—and bewhiles a deep sigh rent her breast.

Sylph-like and ethereal in her beauty, she scarcely seemed to breathe.

In fact she hardly did.

Willowy and slender in form, she was as graceful as a meridian of longitude. Her body seemed almost too frail for motion, while her features were of a mould so delicate as to preclude all thought of intellectual operation.

She was begirt with a flowing kirtle of deep

blue, bebound with a belt bebuckled with a silvern clasp, while about her waist a stomacher of point-lace ended in the ruffled farthingale at her throat. On her head she bore a sugar-loaf hat shaped like an extinguisher and pointing backward at an angle of forty-five degrees.

" Guido," she murmured, " Guido."

And erstwhile she would wring her hands as one distraught and mutter, " He cometh not."

The sun sank and night fell, enwrapping in shadow the frowning castle of Buggensberg, and the ancient city of Ghent at its foot. And as the darkness gathered, the windows of the castle shone out with fiery red, for it was Yuletide, and it was wassail all in the Great Hall of the castle, and this night the Margrave of Buggensberg made him a feast, and celebrated the betrothal of Isolde, his daughter, with Tancred the Tenspot.

And to the feast he had bidden all his liege lords and vassals—Hubert the Husky, Edward the Ear-wig, Rollo the Rumbottle, and many others.

In the meantime the Lady Isolde stood upon the battlements and mourned for the absent Guido.

The love of Guido and Isolde was of that pure and almost divine type, found only in the Middle Ages.

They had never seen one another. Guido had

never seen Isolde, Isolde had never seen Guido.
They had never heard one another speak. They
had never been together. They did not know one
another.

Yet they loved.

Their love had sprung into being suddenly and
romantically, with all the mystic charm which is
love's greatest happiness.

Years before, Guido had seen the name of Isolde
the Slender painted on a fence.

He had turned pale, fallen into a swoon, and
started at once for Jerusalem.

On the very same day Isolde in passing through
the streets of Ghent had seen the Coat of Arms of
Guido hanging on a clothes-line.

She had fallen back into the arms of her tire-
women more dead than alive.

Since that day they had loved.

Isolde would wander forth from the castle at
earliest morn, with the name of Guido on her lips.
She told his name to the trees. She whispered it
to the flowers. She breathed it to the birds. Quite
a lot of them knew it. At times she would ride her
palfrey along the sands of the sea and call
" Guido " to the waves! At other times she would
tell it to the grass or even to a stick of cordwood
or a ton of coal.

Guido and Isolde, though they had never met, cherished each the features of the other. Beneath his coat of mail Guido carried a miniature of Isolde, carven on ivory. He had found it at the bottom of the castle crag, between the castle and the old town of Ghent at its foot.

> How did he know that it was Isolde?
> There was no need for him to ask.
> His heart had spoken.
> The eye of love cannot be deceived.

And Isolde? She, too, cherished beneath her stomacher a miniature of Guido the Gimlet. She had it of a travelling chapman in whose pack she had discovered it, and had paid its price in pearls. How had she known that he it was, that is, that it was he? Because of the Coat of Arms emblazoned beneath the miniature. The same heraldic design that had first shaken her to the heart. Sleeping or waking, it was ever before her eyes: A lion, proper, quartered in a field of gules, and a dog, improper, three-quarters in a field of buckwheat.

And if the love of Isolde burned thus purely for Guido, the love of Guido burned for Isolde with a flame no less pure.

No sooner had love entered Guido's heart than he had determined to do some great feat of emprise or adventure, some high achievement of derringdo which should make him worthy to woo her.

He placed himself under a vow that he would eat nothing, save only food, and drink nothing, save only liquor, till such season as he should have performed his feat.

For this cause he had at once set out for Jerusalem to kill a Saracen for her. He killed one, quite a large one. Still under his vow, he set out again at once to the very confines of Pannonia determined to kill a Turk for her. From Pannonia he passed into the Highlands of Britain, where he killed her a Caledonian.

Every year and every month Guido performed for Isolde some new achievement of emprise.

And in the meantime Isolde waited.

It was not that suitors were lacking. Isolde the Slender had suitors in plenty to do her lightest hest.

Feats of arms were done daily for her sake. To win her love suitors were willing to vow themselves to perdition. For Isolde's sake, Otto the Otter had cast himself into the sea. Conrad the Cocoanut had hurled himself from the highest battlement of the castle head-first into the mud. Hugo the Hopeless had hanged himself by the waistband to a hickory-tree and had refused all efforts to dislodge him.  For her sake Siegfried the Susceptible had swallowed sulphuric acid.

But Isolde the Slender was heedless of the court thus paid to her.

In vain her stepmother, Agatha the Angular, urged her to marry.  In vain her father, the Margrave of Buggensberg, commanded her to choose the one or the other of the suitors.

Her heart remained unswervingly true to the Gimlet.

From time to time love tokens passed between the lovers.  From Jerusalem Guido had sent to her a stick with a notch in it to signify his undying constancy.  From Pannonia he sent a piece of board, and from Venetia about two feet of scantling.  All these Isolde treasured.  At night they lay beneath her pillow.  Then, after years of wandering, Guido had determined to crown his love with a final achievement for Isolde's sake.

It was his design to return to Ghent, to scale by night the castle cliff and to prove his love for Isolde by killing her father for her, casting her stepmother from the battlements, burning the castle, and carrying her away.

This design he was now hastening to put into execution.  Attended by fifty trusty followers under the head of Carlo the Corkscrew and Beo-

wulf the Bradawl, he had made his way to Ghent.
Under cover of night they had reached the foot of
the castle cliff; and now, on their hands and knees
in single file, they were crawling round and round
the spiral path that led up to the gate of the for-
tress. At six of the clock they had spiralled once.
At seven of the clock they had reappeared at the
second round, and as the feast in the hall reached
its height, they reappeared on the fourth lap.

Guido the Gimlet was in the lead. His coat of
mail was hidden beneath a parti-colored cloak
and he bore in his hand a horn.

By arrangement he was to penetrate into the
castle by the postern gate in disguise, steal from the
Margrave by artifice the key of the great door, and
then by a blast of his horn summon his followers to
the assault. Alas! there was need for haste, for at
this very Yuletide, on this very night, the Margrave, wearied of Isolde's resistance, had determined to bestow her hand upon Tancred the Tenspot.

It was wassail all in the great hall. The huge
Margrave, seated at the head of the board, drained
flagon after flagon of wine, and pledged deep the
health of Tancred the Tenspot, who sat plumed and
armored beside him.

Great was the merriment of the Margrave, for

beside him, crouched upon the floor, was a new jester, whom the seneschal had just admitted by the postern gate, and the novelty of whose jests made the huge sides of the Margrave shake and shake again.

" Odds Bodkins! " he roared, " but the tale is as rare as it is new! and so the wagoner said to the Pilgrim that sith he had asked him to put him off the wagon at that town, put him off he must, albeit it was but the small of the night—by St. Pancras! whence hath the fellow so novel a tale?— nay, tell it me but once more, happily I may re- member it "—and the Baron fell back in a perfect paroxysm of merriment.

As he fell back, Guido—for the disguised jester was none other than he, that is, than him—sprang forward and seized from the girdle of the Margrave the key of the great door that dangled at his waist.

Then, casting aside the jester's cloak and cap, he rose to his full height, standing in his coat of mail.

In one hand he brandished the double-headed mace of the Crusader, and in the other a horn.

The guests sprang to their feet, their hands upon their daggers.

" Guido the Gimlet! " they cried.

" Hold," said Guido, " I have you in my power! "

Then placing the horn to his lips and drawing a deep breath, he blew with his utmost force.

And then again he blew—blew like anything.

Not a sound came.

The horn wouldn't blow!

" Seize him! " cried the Baron.

" Stop," said Guido, " I claim the laws of chivalry. I am here to seek the Lady Isolde, betrothed by you to Tancred. Let me fight Tancred in single combat, man to man."

A shout of approbation gave consent.

The combat that followed was terrific.

First Guido, raising his mace high in the air with both hands, brought it down with terrible force on Tancred's mailed head. Then Guido stood still, and Tancred raising his mace in the air brought it down upon Guido's head. Then Tancred stood still and turned his back, and Guido, swinging his mace sideways, gave him a terrific blow from behind, midway, right centre. Tancred returned the blow. Then Tancred knelt down on his hands and knees and Guido brought the mace down on his back. It was a sheer contest of skill and agility. For a time the issue was doubtful. Then Tancred's armor began to bend, his blows weakened, he fell prone. Guido pressed his advantage and hammered him out as flat as a sardine can. Then placing his foot on Tancred's chest, he lowered his vizor and looked around about him.

At this second there was a resounding shriek.

Isolde the Slender, alarmed by the sound of the blows, precipitated herself into the room.

For a moment the lovers looked into each other's faces.

Then with their countenances distraught with agony they fell swooning in different directions.

There had been a mistake!

Guido was not Guido and Isolde was not Isolde. They were wrong about the miniatures. Each of them was a picture of somebody else.

Torrents of remorse flooded over the lovers' hearts.

Isolde thought of the unhappy Tancred, hammered out as flat as a picture-card and hopelessly spoilt; of Conrad the Cocoanut head first in the mud, and Siegfried the Susceptible coiled up with agonies of sulphuric acid.

Guido thought of the dead Saracens and the slaughtered Turks.

And all for nothing!

The guerdon of their love had proved vain. Each of them was not what the other had thought. So it is ever with the loves of this world, and therein is the medieval allegory of this tale.

The hearts of the two lovers broke together.
They expired.

Meantime Carlo the Corkscrew and Beowulf the
Bradawl, and their forty followers, were hustling
down the spirals as fast as they could crawl.

# THE WONDERFUL " ONE-HOSS SHAY "

### Oliver Wendell Holmes

Have you heard of the wonderful one-hoss shay,
That was built in such a logical way
It ran a hundred years to a day,
And then, of a sudden, It—ah, but stay,
I'll tell you what happened without delay,
Scaring the parson into fits,
Frightening the people out of their wits,—
Have you ever heard of that, I say?

Seventeen hundred and fifty-five,
Georgius Secundus was then alive,—
Snuffy old drone from the German hive,
That was the year when Lisbon-town
Saw the earth open and gulp her down,
And Braddock's army was done so brown,
Left without a scalp to its crown.
It was on the terrible Earthquake-day
That the Deacon finished the one-hoss shay.

Now in building of chaises I tell you what,
There is always *somewhere* a weakest spot,—
In hub, tire, felloe, in spring or thill,
In panel, or crossbar, or floor, or sill,

In screw, bolt thoroughbrace,—lurking still,
Find it somewhere you must and will,—
Above or below, or within or without,—
And that's the reason, beyond a doubt,
That a chaise *breaks down*, but doesn't *wear out*.

But the Deacon swore (as Deacons do,
With an " I dew vum," or " I tell yeou ")
He would build one shay to beat the taown
'n' the keounty 'n' all the kentry raoun';
It should be so built that it couldn' break daown:
—" Fur," said the Deacon, " 't's mighty plain
That the weakes' place mus' stan' the strain;
'n' the way t' fix it, uz I maintain, is only jest
T' make that place uz strong uz the rest."

So the Deacon inquired of the village folk
Where he could find the strongest oak,
That couldn't be split nor bent nor broke,—
That was for spokes and floor and sills;
He sent for lancewood to make the thills;
The crossbars were ash, from the straightest
    trees,
The panels of white-wood, that cuts like cheese,
But lasts like iron for things like these;
The hubs of logs from the " Settler's ellum,"—
Last of its timber,—they couldn't sell 'em,

Never an axe had seen their chips,
And the wedges flew from between their lips,
Their blunt ends frizzled like celery-tips;
Step and prop-iron, bolt and screw,
Spring, tire axle, and linch-pin too,
Steel of the finest, bright and blue;
Thoroughbrace bison-skin, thick and wide;
Boot, top, dasher, from tough old hide
Found in the pit when the tanner died.
That was the way he " put her through,"—
" There," said the Deacon, " naow she'll dew! "

Do!   I tell you, I rather guess
She was a wonder, and nothing less!
Colts grew horses, beards turned gray,
Deacon and deaconess dropped away,
Children and grandchildren—where were they?
But there stood the stout old one-hoss shay
As fresh as on Lisbon-earthquake day!

EIGHTEEN HUNDRED;—it came and found
The Deacon's masterpiece strong and sound.
Eighteen hundred increased by ten:—
" Hahnsum kerridge " they called it then.
Eighteen hundred and twenty came;—
Running as usual; much the same.
Thirty and forty at last arrive,
And then came fifty, and FIFTY-FIVE.

Little of all we value here
Wakes on the morn' of its hundredth year
Without both feeling and looking queer.
In fact, there's nothing that keeps its youth,
As far as I know, but a tree and truth.
(This is a moral that runs at large;
Take it.—You're welcome.—No extra charge.)

First of NOVEMBER, the Earthquake day—
There are traces of age in the one-hoss shay,
A general flavor of mild decay,
But nothing local, as one may say.
There couldn't be,—for the Deacon's art
Had made it so like in every part
That there wasn't a chance for one to start;
For the wheels were just as strong as the thills,
And the floor was just as strong as the sills,
And the panels just as strong as the floor,
And the whipple-tree neither less nor more,
And the back-crossbar as strong as the fore,
And spring and axle and nub *encore*.
And yet, *as a whole,* it is past a doubt
In another hour it will be *worn out!*

First of November, 'Fifty-five!
This morning the parson takes a drive.
Now, small boys, get out of the way!
Here comes the wonderful one-hoss shay,

Drawn by a rat-tailed, ewe-necked bay.
" Huddup! " said the parson.—Off went they.
The parson was working his Sunday's text,
Had got to *fifthly,* and stopped perplexed
At what the—Moses—was coming next.
All at once the horse stood still,
Close by the meet'n'-house on the hill.
—First a shiver, and then a thrill,
Then something decidedly like a spill,—
And the parson was sitting on a rock,
At half-past nine by the meet'n'-house clock,—
Just the hour of the Earthquake shock!
—What do you think the parson found,
When he got up and stared around?
The poor old chaise in a heap or mound,
As if it had been to the mill and ground!
You see, of course, if you're not a dunce,
How it went to pieces all at once,—
All at once and nothing first,—
Just as bubbles do when they burst.

End of the wonderful one-hoss shay,
Logic is logic.   That's all I say.

# A CHAPTER FROM "MARTIN CHUZZLEWIT,"

## THE BURDEN WHEREOF IS HAIL COLUMBIA

### CHARLES DICKENS

" ONWARD she comes, in gallant combat with the elements, her tall masts trembling, and her timbers starting on the strain; onward she comes, now high upon the curling billows, now low down in the hollows of the sea, as hiding for the moment from its fury; and every storm-voice in the air and water, cries more loudly yet, ' A ship! '

" And though the eager multitude crowd thick and fast upon her all the night, and dawn of day discovers the untiring train yet bearing down upon the ship in an eternity of troubled water, onward she comes, with dim lights burning in her hull, and people there asleep; as if no deadly element were peering in at every seam and chink, and no drowned seaman's grave, with but a plank to cover it, were yawning in the unfathomable depths below.

" Among these sleeping voyagers were Martin and Mark Tapley, who, rocked into a heavy drowsiness by the unaccustomed motion, were as insensible to the foul air in which they lay, as to the uproar without. It was broad day, when the latter awoke with a dim idea that he was dreaming of having gone to sleep in a four-post bedstead which had turned bottom-upwards in the course of the night. There was more reason in this, too, than in the roasting of eggs; for the first objects Mr. Tapley recognized when he opened his eyes were his own heels—looking down at him, as he afterwards observed, from a nearly perpendicular elevation.

" ' Well!' said Mark, getting himself into a sitting posture, after various ineffectual struggles with the rolling of the ship. ' This is the first time as ever I stood on my head all night.'

" ' You shouldn't go to sleep upon the ground with your head to leeward, then,' growled a man in one of the berths.

" ' With my head to where?' asked Mark.

" The man repeated his previous sentiment.

" ' No, I won't another time,' said Mark, ' when I know whereabouts on the map that country is. In the meanwhile I can give you a better piece of advice. Don't you nor any other friend of mine never go to sleep with his head in a ship, any more.'

" The man gave a grunt of discontented acquiescence, turning over in his berth, and drew his blanket over his head.

" ' For,' said Mr. Tapley, pursuing the theme by way of soliloquy, in a low tone of voice, ' the sea is as nonsensical a thing as any going. It never knows what to do with itself. It hasn't got no employment for its mind, and is always in a state of vacancy. Like them Polar bears in the wild-beast-shows as is constantly a-nodding their heads from side to side, it never can be quiet. Which is entirely owing to its uncommon stupidity.'

" ' Is that you, Mark?' asked a faint voice from another berth.

" ' It's as much of me as is left, sir, after a fort-night of this work,' Mr. Tapley replied. ' What with leading the life of a fly, ever since I've been aboard—for I've been perpetually holding on to something or other, in a upside-down position—what with that, sir, and putting a very little into myself, and taking a good deal out of myself, there ain't too much of me to swear by. How do you find yourself this morning, sir? '

" ' Very miserable,' said Martin, with a peevish groan. ' Ugh! This is wretched, indeed! '

" ' Creditable,' muttered Mark, pressing one hand upon his aching head and looking round him with a rueful grin. ' That's the great comfort. It is creditable to keep up one's spirits here. Virtue's its own reward. So's jollity.'

" Mark was so far right, that unquestionably any man who retained his cheerfulness among the steerage accommodations of that noble and fast-sailing line-of-packet ship, the *Screw,* was solely indebted to his own resources, and shipped his good humor, like his provisions, without any contribution or assistance from the owners. A dark, low, stifling cabin, surrounded by berths all filled to overflowing with men, women, and children, in various stages of sickness and misery, is not the liveliest place of assembly at any time; but when it is so crowded (as the steerage cabin of the *Screw* was, every passage out,) that mattresses and beds are heaped upon the floor, to the extinction of everything like comfort, cleanliness, and decency, it is liable to operate not only as a pretty strong barrier against amiability of temper, but as a positive encourager of selfish and rough humors. Mark felt this, as he sat looking about him, and his spirits rose proportionately. Mark looked about him wistfully, and his face brightened as he looked. Here an old grandmother was crooning over a sick child, and rocking it to and fro, in arms hardly more wasted than its own young limbs; here a poor woman with an infant in her lap, mended another little creature's clothes, and quieted another who was creeping up about her from their scanty bed upon the floor. Here were old men awkwardly engaged in little household offices, wherein they would have been ridiculous but for their good-will and kind purpose; and here were swarthy fellows—giants in their way— doing such little acts of tenderness for those about them, as might have belonged to gentlest-hearted dwarfs. The very idiot in the corner who sat mowing there, all day, had his faculty of imitation roused by what he saw about him; and snapped his fingers, to amuse a crying child.

" ' Now then,' said Mark, nodding to a woman who was dressing her three children at no great distance from him—and the grin upon his face had by this time spread from ear to ear—' hand over one of them young uns according to custom.'

" ' I wish you'd get breakfast, Mark, instead of worrying with people who don't belong to you,' observed Martin, petulantly.

" ' All right,' said Mark. ' She'll do that. It's fair division of labor, sir. I wash her boys, and she makes our tea. I never could make tea, but any one can wash a boy.'

" The woman, who was delicate and ill, felt and understood his kindness, as well she might, for she had been covered every night with his greatcoat, while he had had for his own bed the bare boards and a rug. But Martin, who seldom got up or looked about him, was quite incensed by the folly of this speech, and expressed his dissatisfaction by an impatient groan.

" ' So it is, certainly,' said Mark, brushing the child's hair as coolly as if he had been born and bred a barber.

" ' What are you talking about now?' asked Martin.

" ' What you said,' replied Mark, ' or what you meant, when you gave that there dismal vent to your feelings. I quite go along with you, sir. It is very hard upon her.'

" ' What is?'

" ' Making the voyage by herself along with these young impediments here, and going such a way at such a time of the year to join her husband. If you don't want to be driven mad with yellow soap in your eye, young man,' said Mr. Tapley to the second urchin, who was by this time under his hands at the basin, ' you'd better shut it.'

" ' Where does she join her husband?' asked Martin, yawning.

" ' Why, I'm very much afraid,' said Mr. Tapley, in a low voice, ' that she don't know. I hope she mayn't miss him. But she sent her last letter by hand, and it don't seem to have been very clearly

understood between 'em without it, and if she don't
see him a-waving his pocket-handkerchief on the
shore, like a picture out of a song book, my opinion
is she'll break her heart.'

" ' Why, how, in Folly's name, does the woman
come to be on board ship on such a wild goose
venture? ' cried Martin.

" Mr. Tapley glanced at him for a moment as he
lay prostrate in his berth, and then said, very
quietly,—'Ah! How, indeed! I can't think.
He's been away from her for two years; she's been
very poor and lonely in her own country; and has
always been a-looking forward to meeting him.
It's very strange she should be here.   Quite amazing!   A little mad, perhaps!   There can't be no
other way of accounting for it.'

" It is due to Mark Tapley to state, that he
suffered at least as much from sea-sickness as any
man, woman, or child, on board; and that he had a
peculiar faculty of knocking himself about on the
smallest provocation, and losing his legs at every
lurch of the ship.   But resolved, in his usual
phrase, to ' come out strong ' under disadvanta-
geous circumstances, he was the life and soul of the
steerage, and made no more of stopping in the
middle of a facetious conversation to go away and
be excessively ill by himself, and afterwards come

back in the very best and gayest of tempers to re-
sume it, than if such a course of proceeding had
been the commonest in the world.

" It cannot be said that as his illness wore off, his
cheerfulness and good-nature increased, because
they would hardly admit of augmentation; but his
usefulness among the weaker members of the party
was much enlarged; and at all times and seasons
there he was exerting it. If a gleam of sun shone
out of the dark sky, down Mark tumbled into the
cabin, and presently up he came again with a
woman in his arms, or half a dozen children, or a
man, or a bed, or a saucepan, or a basket, or something animate or inanimate, that he thought would
be the better for the air. In short, there never was
a more popular character than Mark Tapley became, on board that noble and fast-sailing line-of-
packet ship, the *Screw;* and he attained at last to
such a pitch of universal admiration, that he began
to have grave doubts within himself whether a man
might reasonably claim any credit for being jolly
under such exciting circumstances.

" ' Well, Mark,' said Martin, near whose berth he
had ruminated to this effect, ' when will this be
over? '

" ' Another week, they say, sir,' returned Mark,
' will most likely bring us into port. The ship's

a-going along at present, as sensible as a ship can, sir; though I don't mean to say as that's any very high praise.'

" ' I don't think it is indeed,' groaned Martin.

" ' You'd feel all the better for it, sir, if you was to turn out,' observed Mark.

" ' And be seen by the ladies and gentlemen on the afterdeck,' returned Martin, with a scornful emphasis upon the words, ' mingling with the beggarly crowd that are stowed away in this vile hole. I should be greatly the better for that, no doubt!'

" ' I'm thankful that I can't say from my own experience what the feelings of a gentleman would be,' said Mark, ' but I should have thought, sir, as a gentleman would feel a deal more uncomfortable down here, than up in the fresh air, especially when the ladies and gentlemen in the after-cabin know just as much about him, as he does about them, and are likely to trouble their heads about him in the same proportion. I should have thought that, certainly.'

" ' I tell you, then,' rejoined Martin, ' you would have thought wrong, and do think wrong.'

" ' Very likely, sir,' said Mark, with imperturbable good temper, ' I often do.'

" ' As to lying here,' cried Martin, raising him-

self on his elbow, and looking angrily at his fol-
lower, ' do you suppose it's a pleasure to lie here? '

" ' All the madhouses in the world,' said Mr.
Tapley, ' couldn't produce such a maniac as the
man must be who could think that.'

" ' Then why are you forever goading and urg-
ing me to get up? ' asked Martin. ' I lie here because I don't wish to be recognized, in the better
days to which I aspire, by any purse-proud citizen,
as the man who came over with him among the
steerage passengers. I lie here, because I wish to
conceal my circumstances and myself, and not to
arrive in a new world badged and ticketed as an
utterly poverty-stricken man. If I could have
afforded a passage in the after-cabin, I should have
held up my head with the rest. As I couldn't, I
hide it. Do you understand that? '

" ' I am very sorry, sir,' said Mark. ' I didn't
know you took it so much to heart as this comes to.'

" ' Of course you didn't know,' returned his
master. ' How should you know, unless I told
you? It's no trial to you, Mark, to make yourself
comfortable and to bustle about. It's as natural
for you to do so under the circumstances as it is for
me not to do so. Why, you don't suppose there is
a living creature in this ship who can by possibility
have half so much to undergo on board of her as I

have.  Do you?' he asked, sitting upright in his
berth and looking at Mark, with an expression of
great earnestness not unmixed with wonder.

"Mark twisted his face into a tight knot, and
with his head very much on one side pondered upon
this question as if he felt it an extremely difficult
one to answer.

"And now a general excitement began to prevail
on board; and various predictions relative to the
precise day, and even the precise hour, at which
they would reach New York, were freely broached.
There was infinitely more crowding on deck and
looking over the ship's side than there had been
before; and an epidemic broke out for packing up
things every morning, which required unpacking
again every night.  Those who had any letters to
deliver, or any friends to meet, or any settled plans
of going anywhere or doing anything, discussed
their prospects a hundred times a day; and as this
class of passengers was very small, and the number
of those who had no prospects whatever was very
large, there were plenty of listeners and few talkers.
Those who had been ill all along, got well now, and
those who had been well got better.  An American
gentleman in the after-cabin, who had been
wrapped up in fur and oilskin the whole passage,
unexpectedly appeared in a very shiny, tall, black

hat, and constantly overhauled a very little valise of pale leather, which contained his clothes, linen, brushes, shaving apparatus, books, trinkets, and other baggage. He likewise stuck his hands deep into his pockets, and walked the deck with his nostrils dilated, as already inhaling the air of Freedom which carries death to all tyrants, and can never (under any circumstances worth mentioning) be breathed by slaves. An English gentleman who was strongly suspected of having run away from a bank, with something in his possession belonging to its strong box, besides the key, grew eloquent upon the subject of the rights of man, and hummed the Marseillaise Hymn constantly. In a word, one great sensation pervaded the whole ship, and the soil of America lay close before them; so close at last, that, upon a certain starlight night, they took a pilot on board, and within a few hours afterwards lay to until the morning, awaiting the arrival of a steamboat in which the passengers were to be conveyed ashore.

" Off she came, soon after it was light next morning, and, lying alongside an hour or more— during which period her very firemen were objects of hardly less interest and curiosity, than if they had been so many angels, good or bad,—took all her living freight aboard. Among them, Mark, who still had his friend and her three children under his close protection; and Martin, who had once more dressed himself in his usual attire, but wore a soiled old cloak above his ordinary clothes, until such time as he should separate forever from his late companions.

" The steamer—which, with its machinery on deck, looked, as it worked its long slim legs, like some enormously magnified insect or antediluvian monster—dashed at great speed up a beautiful bay; and presently they saw some heights, and islands, and a long flat, straggling city.

" ' And this,' said Mr. Tapley, looking far ahead, ' is the Land of Liberty, is it? Very well, I'm agreeable. Any land will do for me after so much water! ' "

*—Abridged.*

# THE HEIGHT OF THE RIDICULOUS

OLIVER WENDELL HOLMES

I WROTE some lines once on a time,
  In wondrous merry mood,
And thought, as usual, men would say
  They were exceeding good.

They were so queer, so very queer,
  I laughed as I would die:
Albeit, in the general way,
  A sober man am I.

I called my servant, and he came:
  How kind it was of him,
To mind a slender man like me,
  He of the mighty limb!

"These to the printer," I exclaimed,
  And, in my humorous way,
I added (as a trifling jest),
  "There'll be the devil to pay."

He took the paper, and I watched,
   And saw him peep within:
At the first line he read, his face
   Was all upon the grin.

He read the next: the grin grew broad,
   And shot from ear to ear:
He read the third: a chuckling noise
   I now began to hear.

The fourth: he broke into a roar:
   The fifth: his waistband split:
The sixth: he burst five buttons off,
   And tumbled in a fit.

Ten days and nights, with sleepless eye,
   I watched that wretched man,
And since, I never dare to write
   As funny as I can.

# THE MAYOR OF SCUTTLETON

### Mary Mapes Dodge

The Mayor of Scuttleton burned his nose
Trying to warm his copper toes;
He lost his money and spoiled his will
By signing his name with an icicle quill:
He went bareheaded, and held his breath,
And frightened his grandame 'most to death;
He loaded a shovel and tried to shoot,
And killed the calf in the leg of his boot:
He melted a snowbird and formed the habit
Of dancing jigs with a sad Welsh rabbit:
He lived on taffy and taxed the town:
And read his newspaper upside down.
Then he sighed and hung his hat on a feather,
And bade the townspeople come together:
But the worst of it all was, nobody knew
What the Mayor of Scuttleton next would do.

# THE ORIGIN OF ROAST PIG

## Charles Lamb

MANKIND, says a Chinese manuscript, which my
friend M. was obliging enough to read and explain
to me, for the first seventy thousand ages ate their
meat raw, clawing or biting it from the animal, just
as they do in Abyssinia to this day. . . .
The manuscript goes on to say that the art of roasting, or rather broiling (which I take to be the elder
brother), was accidentally discovered in the manner
following.   The swineherd, Ho-ti, having gone out
into the woods one morning, as his manner was, to
collect mast for his hogs, left his cottage in the care
of his eldest son, Bo-bo, a great lubberly boy, who
being fond of playing with fire, as youngsters of
his age commonly are, let some sparks escape into
a bundle of straw, which, kindling quickly, spread
the conflagration over every part of their poor
mansion, till it was reduced to ashes.   Together
with a cottage (a sorry antediluvian makeshift of a
building, you may think it), which was of more
importance, a fine litter of new-born pigs, no less
than nine in number, perished.   China pigs have
been esteemed a luxury all over the East, from the

remotest periods that we read of. Bo-bo was in the utmost consternation, as you may think, not so much for the sake of the tenement, which his father and he could easily build up again with a few dry branches, and the labor of an hour or two, at any time, as for the loss of the pigs.

While he was thinking what he should say to his father, and wringing his hands over the smoking remnants of one of those untimely sufferers, an odor assailed his nostrils, unlike any scent which he had before experienced. What could it proceed from? Not from the burnt cottage—he had smelt that smell before; indeed this was by no means the first accident of the kind which had occurred through the negligence of this unlucky firebrand. Much less did it resemble that of any known herb, weed or flower. A premonitory moistening at the same time overflowed his nether lip. He knew not what to think. He next stooped down to feel the pig, if there were any signs of life in it. He burned his fingers, and to cool them he applied them in his booby fashion to his mouth. Some of the crumbs of the scorched skin had come away with his fingers, and for the first time in his life (in the world's life, indeed, for before him no man had known it) he tasted—crackling. Again he felt and fumbled at the pig. It did not burn him so much

now; still he licked his fingers from a sort of habit.
The truth at length broke into his slow understanding that it was the pig that smelt so, and the pig
that tasted so delicious; and surrendering himself
up to the new-born pleasure, he fell to tearing up
whole handfuls of the scorched skin with the flesh
next to it, and was cramming it down his throat in
his beastly fashion, when his sire entered amid the
smoking rafters, armed with a retributory cudgel,
and finding how affairs stood, began to rain blows
upon the young rogue's shoulders, as thick as hail-
stones, which Bo-bo heeded not any more than if
they had been flies.  The tickling pleasure which
he experienced in his lower regions had rendered
him quite callous to any inconveniences he might
feel in those remote quarters.  His father might
lay on, but he could not beat him from the pig, till
he had fairly made an end of it, when, becoming a
little sensible of his situation, something like the
following dialogue ensued:

" O father, the pig, the pig!   Do come and taste
how nice the burnt pig eats."

The ears of Ho-ti tingled with horror.  He
cursed his son, and he cursed himself that ever he
should beget a son that should eat burnt pig.

Bo-bo, whose scent was wonderfully sharpened
since the morning, soon raked out another pig, and

fairly rending it asunder, thrust the lesser half by main force into the fists of Ho-ti, still shouting out, "Eat, eat, eat the burnt pig, father. Only taste—O Lord!" With such like barbarous ejaculations, cramming his mouth all the while as if he would choke.

Ho-ti trembled in every joint while he grasped the abominable thing, wavering whether he should not put his son to death for an unnatural young monster, when the crackling scorching his fingers, as it had done his son's, and applying the same remedy to them, he in turn tasted some of its flavor, which, make what sour mouths he would for pretense, proved not altogether displeasing to him. In conclusion (for the manuscript here is a little tedious) both the father and son fairly sat down to the mess, and never left off till they had despatched all that remained of the litter.

Bo-bo was strictly enjoined not to let the secret escape, for the neighbors would certainly have stoned them for a couple of abominable wretches, who could think of improving upon the good meat which God had sent them. Nevertheless, strange stories got about. It was observed that Ho-ti's cottage was burned down more frequently than ever. Nothing but fires from this time forward. Some would break out in broad day, others in the night-time. So often as the sow had young pigs, so sure was the house of Ho-ti to be in a blaze. Ho-ti himself, which was the more remarkable, instead of chastising his son, seemed to grow more indulgent to him than ever. At length they were watched, the terrible mystery discovered, and the father and son summoned to take their trial at Pekin, then an inconsiderable assize town. Evidence was given, the obnoxious food produced in court, and verdict about to be pronounced, when the foreman of the jury begged that some of the burnt pig, of which the culprit stood accused, might be handed into the box. He handled it, and they all handled it, and burning their fingers as Bo-bo and his father had done before them, and nature prompting to each of them the same remedy, against the face of all the facts, and the clearest charge which judge had ever given,—to the surprise of the whole court, townsfolk, strangers, reporters, and all present— without leaving the box, or any manner of consultation whatever, they brought in a simultaneous verdict of Not Guilty.

The judge, who was a shrewd fellow, winked at the manifest iniquity of the decision, and when the court was dismissed, went privily, and bought up all the pigs that could be had for love or money. In a few days his lordship's town house was observed to be on fire. The thing took wing, and now there was nothing to be seen but fire in every direction. Fuel and pigs grew enormously dear all over the district. The insurance offices one and all shut up shop. People built slighter and slighter every day, until it was feared that the very science of architecture would in no long time be lost to the world. Thus this custom of firing houses continued, till in the process of time, says my manuscript, a sage arose, like our Locke, who made a discovery, that the flesh of swine, or indeed of any other animal, might be cooked (burned, as they call it) without the necessity of consuming a whole house to dress it. Then first began the rude form of gridiron. Roasting by the string or spit came in a century or two later, I forget in whose dynasty. By such slow degrees, concludes the manuscript, do the most useful and seemingly the most obvious arts make their way among mankind.

Without placing too implicit faith in the account above given, it must be agreed, that if a worthy pretext for so dangerous an experiment as setting houses on fire (especially in those days) could be assigned in favor of any culinary object, that pretext and excuse might be found in Roast Pig.

# JAILLESS CRIMES:—(*Killing Time*)

## JUDGE

HANGING pictures.
Stealing bases.
Shooting the chutes.
Choking off a speaker.
Running over a new song.
Smothering a laugh.
Setting fire to a heart.
Knifing a performance.
Murdering the English language.

# THE BIGELOW PAPERS.  NO. VII

## James Russell Lowell

Ef I a song or two could make
  Like rockets druv by their own burnin',
All leap an' light, to leave a wake
  Men's hearts an' faces skyward turnin'!—
But, it strikes me, 't ain't jest the time
  Fer stringin' words with settisfaction;
Wut's wanted now's the silent rhyme
  'Twixt upright Will an' downright Action.

Oh, Jon'than, ef you want to be
  A rugged chap agin an' hearty,
Go fer wutever'll hurt Jeff D.,
  Nut wut'll boost up ary party.
Here's hell broke loose, an' we lay flat
  With half the univarse a-singin',
Till Sen'to This an' Governor Thet
  Stop squabblin' fer the garding-ingin.

It's war we're in, not politics;
  It's systems wrastlin' now, not parties;
An' victory in the end'll fix
  Where longest will an' truest heart is.

An' wut's the Guv'ment folks about?
  Tryin' to hope ther's nothin' doin',
An' look ez though they didn't doubt
  Sunthin' pertickler wuz a-brewin'.

Ther's critters yit thet talk an' act
  Fer wut they call Conciliation;
They'd hand a buff'lo-drove a tract
  When they wuz madder than all Bashan.
Conciliate?   It jest means *be kicked,*
  No metter how they phrase an' tone it;
It means thet we're to set down licked,
  Thet we're poor shotes an' glad to own it!

A war on tick's ez dear'z the deuce,
  But it wun't leave no lastin' traces,
Ez't would to make a sneakin' truce
  Without no moral specie-basis;
Ef green-backs ain't nut jest the cheese,
  I guess ther's evils thet's extremer,—
Fer instance,—shinplaster idees
  Like them put out by Guv'nor Seymour.

Last year, the Nation, at a word,
  When tremblin' Freedom cried to shield her,
Flamed weldin' into one keen sword
  Waitin' an' longin' fer a wielder;

A splendid flash!—but how'd the grasp
  With sech a chance ez thet wuz tally?
Ther' warn't no meanin' in our clasp,—
  Half this, half thet, all shilly-shally.

More men!   More men!   It's there we fail;
  Weak plans grow weaker yit by lengthenin';
Wut use in addin' to the tail,
  When it's the head's in need o' strengthenin'?
We wanted one thet felt all Chief
  From roots o' hair to sole o' stockin',
Square-sot, with thousan'-ton belief
  In him an' us, ef earth went rockin'!

Ole Hick'ry wouldn't ha' stood see-saw
  'Bout doin' things till they wuz done with,—
He'd smashed the tables o' the Law
  In time o' need to load his gun with;
He couldn't see but jest one side,—
  Ef his, 'twuz God's, an' thet wuz plenty;
An' so his " Forrards! " multiplied
  An army's fightin' weight by twenty.

But this 'ere histin', creak, creak, creak,
  Your cappen's heart up with a derrick,
This tryin' to coax a lightin'-streak
  Out of a half-discouraged hay-rick,

This hangin' on mont' arter mont'
    Fer one sharp purpose 'mongst the twitter,—
I tell ye, it doos kind o' stunt
    The peth and sperit of a critter.


In six months where'll the People be,
    Ef leaders look on revolution
Ez though it wuz a cup o' tea,—
    Jest social el'ments in solution?
This weighin' things doos wal enough
    When war cools down, an' comes to writin';
But while it's makin' the true stuff
    Is pison, mad, pig-headed fightin'.


Democ'acy gives every man
    The right to be his own oppressor;
But a loose Gov'ment ain't the plan,
    Helpless ez spilled beans on a dresser;
I tell ye one thing critters, the Seceders,—
    Ef bein' right's the fust consarn,
The 'fore-the-fust's cast-iron leaders.


But 'pears to me I see some signs
    Thet we're a-goin' to use our senses;
Jeff druv us into these hard lines,
    An' ough' to bear his half th' expenses;

Slavery's Secession's heart an' will,
　　South, North, East, West, where'er you find
　　　　it,
An' ef it drops into War's mill,
　　D' ye say them thunder-stones sha'n't grind
　　　　it?


D' ye s'pose, ef Jeff giv *him* a lick,
　　Ole Hick'ry 'd tried his head to sof'n
So 's 't wouldn't hurt thet ebony stick
　　Thet 's made our side see stars so of'n?
" No! " he'd ha' thundered, " On your knees,
　　An' own one flag, one road to glory!
Soft-heartedness, in times like these,
　　Shows sof'ness in the upper story! "


An' why should we kick up a muss
　　About the Pres'dunt's proclamation?
It ain't a-goin' to lib'rate us,
　　Ef we don't like emancipation;
The right to be a cussed fool
　　Is safe from all devices human,
It's common (ez a gin'l rule)
　　To every critter born o' woman.

So *we*'re all right, an' I, fer one,
    Don't think our cause 'll lose in vally
By rammin' Scriptur' in our gun,
    An' gittin' Natur' fer an ally;
Thank God, say I, fer even a plan
    To lift one human bein's level,
Give one more chance to make a man,
    Or, anyhow, to spile a devil!


Not thet I'm one thet much expec'
    Millennium by express to-morrow;
They *will* miscarry,—I rec'lec'
    Tu many on 'em, to my sorrer;
Men ain't made angels in a day,
    No matter how you mould an' labor 'em,—
Nor 'riginal ones, I guess, don't stay
    With Abe so of'n ez with Abraham.


The'ry thinks Fact a pooty thing,
    An' wants the banns read right ensuin';
But fact wun't noways wear the ring,
    'Thout years o' settin' up an' wooin';
Though, arter all, Time's dial-plate
    Marks cent'ries with the minute-finger,
An' God can't never come tu late,
    Though it does seem to try an' linger.

An' come wut will, I think it's grand
  Abe's gut his will et last bloom-furnaced
In trial-flames till it'll stand
  The strain o' bein' in deadly earnest;
Thet's wut we want,—we want to know
  The folks on our side hez the bravery
To b'lieve ez hard, come weal, come woe,
  In Freedom ez Jeff doos in Slavery.

Set the two forces foot to foot,
  An' every man knows who'll be winner,
Whose faith in God hez ary root
  Thet goes down deeper than his dinner;
*Then* 't will be felt from pole to pole,
  Without no need o' proclamation,
Earth's biggest Country's gut her soul
  An' risen up Earth's Greatest Nation!

# HOW TO TELL THE WILD FLOWERS

### Carolyn Wells

### *The Saratoga Trunk*

The Saratoga Trunk I find
  To be the largest of its kind.
'Tis old and hollow, and perhaps
  That's why it's fastened round with straps;
But look inside—it seems to be
  The trunk of some old family tree.

### *The Square Root*

The Square Root is not nice a bit.
  Mathematicians dig for it;
They seem to relish it, but I
  Think it exceedingly hard and dry.
Yet 'tis of use, for I suppose
  From it a branch of learning grows.

### *The Electric-Light Plant*

Here's the Electric-Light Plant; see
  How bright its blossoms seem to be.
Afar it spreads its branching routes;
  Electric currents are its fruits.
It is a house-plant; in our rooms
  We may enjoy its brilliant blooms.

## The Society Bud

A house-plant;—in a heated room
This little bud is forced to bloom;
'Tis young and small and somewhat green,
    Close to the parent stem 'tis seen,
And if it ventures but to speak,
    A blush comes to its soft, pink cheek.

## Fly-Leaves

Of surface smooth and texture fine,
    These leaves have neither vein nor line.
They're found in groups of two or three:
    Of little use they seem to be.
Even in autumn, it is said,
    Though they may turn, they are not read.

## Wild Oats

Wild Oats are sown by many a fop,
    Who is dismayed to see the crop.
He goes to threshing with a vim,
    (The threshing should be given to him!)
Alas! the oats he can't remove—
    A food for nightmares oft they prove.

# FAITHLESS NELLY GRAY
## (*A PATHETIC BALLAD*)

### Thomas Hood

Ben Battle was a soldier bold,
   And used to war's alarms:
But a cannon-ball took off his legs,
   So he laid down his arms!

Now as they bore him off the field,
   Said he, " Let others shoot,
For here I leave my second leg
   And the forty-second Foot! "

The army-surgeons made him limbs;
   Said he,—" They're only pegs:
But there's as wooden members quite,
   As represent my legs! "

Now Ben he loved a pretty maid,
   Her name was Nelly Gray;
So he went to pay her his devours,
   When he'd devour'd his pay!

But when he called on Nelly Gray,
    She made him quite a scoff;
And when she saw his wooden legs,
    Began to take them off!

" Oh, Nelly Gray!   Oh, Nelly Gray!
    Is this your love so warm?
The love that loves a scarlet coat
    Should be more uniform! "

Said she, " I loved a soldier once,
    For he was blithe and brave;
But I will never have a man
    With both legs in the grave!

" Before you had those timber toes,
    Your love I did allow,
But then, you know, you stand upon
    Another footing now! "

" Oh, Nelly Gray!   Oh, Nelly Gray!
    For all your jeering speeches,
At duty's call, I left my legs
    In Badajos's breaches! "

" Why, then," said she, " you've lost the feet
    Of legs in war's alarms,
And now you cannot wear your shoes
    Upon your feats of arms! "

" Oh, false and fickle Nelly Gray!
　　I know why you refuse:
Though I've no feet, some other man
　　Is standing in my shoes!

" I wish I ne'er had seen your face:
　　But, now, a long farewell!
For you will be my death,—alas!
　　You will not be my Nell! "

Now when he went from Nelly Gray,
　　His heart so heavy got—
And life was such a burden grown,
　　It made him take a knot!

So round his melancholy neck
　　A rope he did entwine,
And, for his second time in life,
　　Enlisted in the Line!

One end he tied around a beam,
　　And then removed his pegs,
And, as his legs were off,—of course,
　　He soon was off his legs!

And there he hung, till he was dead
　　As any nail in town,
For though distress had cut him up,
　　It could not cut him down!

# THE WONDERFUL OLD MAN

THERE was an old man
   Who lived on a common
And, if fame speaks true,
   He was born of a woman.
Perhaps you will laugh,
   But for truth I've been told
He once was an infant
   Tho' age made him old.

Whene'er he was hungry
   He longed for some meat;
And if he could get it
   'Twas said he would eat.
When thirsty he'd drink
   If you gave him a pot,
And what he drank mostly
   Ran down his throat.

He seldom or never
   Could see without light,
And yet I've been told he
   Could hear in the night.
He has oft been awake
   In the daytime, 'tis said,
And has fallen asleep
   As he lay in his bed.

'Tis reported his tongue
   Always moved when he talk'd,
And he stirred both his arms
   And his legs when he walk'd;
And his gait was so odd
   Had you seen him you'd burst,
For one leg or t'other
   Would always be first.

His face was the drollest
   That ever was seen,
For if 'twas not washed
   It seldom was clean;
His teeth he expos'd when
   He happened to grin,
And his mouth stood across
   'Twixt his nose and his chin.

When this whimsical chap
   Had a river to pass,
If he couldn't get over
   He stayed where he was.
'Tis said he ne'er ventured
   To quit the dry ground,
Yet so great was his luck
   He never was drowned.

At last he fell sick,
  As old chronicles tell,
And then, as folks say,
  He was not very well.
But what was as strange
  In so weak a condition,
As he could not give fees
  He could get no physician.

What wonder he died!
  Yet 'tis said that his death
Was occasioned at last
  By the loss of his breath.
But peace to his bones
  Which in ashes now moulder.
Had he lived a day longer
  He'd have been a day older.

# QUEEN ALICE
### (*From Through the Looking-Glass.*)

## CHARLES LUTWIDGE DODGSON
### (*Lewis Carroll*)

"WELL, this *is* grand!" said Alice. "I never expected I should be a Queen so soon—and I'll tell you what it is, your majesty," she went on in a severe tone (she was always rather fond of scolding herself), "it'll never do for you to be lolling about on the grass like that! Queens have to be dignified, you know!"

So she got up and walked about—rather stiffly just at first, as she was afraid that the crown might come off: but she comforted herself with the thought that there was nobody to see her, "and if I really am a Queen," she said, as she sat down again, "I shall be able to manage it quite well in time."

Everything was happening so oddly that she didn't feel a bit surprised at finding the Red Queen and the White Queen sitting close to her, one on each side: she would have liked very much to ask them how they came there, but she feared it would not be quite civil. However, there would be no harm, she thought, in asking if the game was over.

"Please, would you tell me ——" she began, looking timidly at the Red Queen.

"Speak when you're spoken to!" the Queen sharply interrupted her.

"But if everybody obeyed that rule," said Alice, who was always ready for a little argument, "and if you only spoke when you were spoken to, and the other person always waited for *you* to begin, you see nobody would ever say anything, so that ——"

"Ridiculous!" cried the Queen. "Why, don't you see, child ——" here she broke off with a frown, and, after thinking for a minute, suddenly changed the subject of the conversation. "What do you mean by ' If you really are a Queen?' What right have you to call yourself so? You can't be a Queen, you know, till you've passed the proper examination. And the sooner we begin it, the better."

"I only said ' if,' " poor Alice pleaded in a piteous tone.

The two Queens looked at each other, and the Red Queen remarked, with a little shudder, "She *says* she only said ' if ' ——"

"But she said a great deal more than that," the

White Queen moaned, wringing her hands. " Oh, ever so much more than that."

" So you did, you know," the Red Queen said to Alice. " Always speak the truth—think before you speak—and write it down afterwards."

" I'm sure I didn't mean ——" Alice was beginning, but the Red Queen interrupted her impatiently.

" That's just what I complain of. You *should* have meant! What do you suppose is the use of a child without any meaning? Even a joke should have some meaning—and a child's more important than a joke, I hope. You couldn't deny that, even if you tried with both hands."

" I don't deny things with my *hands*," Alice objected.

" Nobody said you did," said the Red Queen. " I said you couldn't if you tried."

" She's in that state of mind," said the White Queen, " that she wants to deny *something*—only she doesn't know what to deny."

" A nasty, vicious temper," the Red Queen remarked; and then there was an uncomfortable silence for a minute or two.

The Red Queen broke the silence by saying to the White Queen, " I invite you to Alice's dinner-party this afternoon."

The White Queen smiled feebly, and said, " And I invite *you*."

" I didn't know I was to have a party at all," said Alice, " but if there is to be one, I think *I* ought to invite the guests."

" We gave you the opportunity of doing it," tne Red Queen remarked; " but I dare say you've not had many lessons in manners yet."

" Manners are not taught in lessons," said Alice. " Lessons teach you to do sums, and things of that sort."

" Can you do Addition?" the White Queen asked. " What's one and one and one and one and one and one and. one and one and one and one?"

" I don't know," said Alice. " I lost count."

" She can't do Addition," the Red Queen interrupted. " Can you do Subtraction? Take nine from eight."

" Nine from eight I can't, you know," Alice replied very readily; " but ——"

" She can't do Subtraction," said the White Queen. " Can you do Division? Divide a loaf by a knife—what's the answer to that?"

" I suppose ——" Alice was beginning, but the Red Queen answered for her.

" Bread-and-butter, of course. Try another Subtraction sum. Take a bone from a dog: what remains?"

Alice considered. "The bone wouldn't remain, of course, if I took it—and the dog wouldn't remain; it would come to bite me—and I'm sure I shouldn't remain!"

"Then you think nothing would remain?" said the Red Queen.

"I think that's the answer."

"Wrong as usual," said the Red Queen. "The dog's temper would remain."

"But I don't see how ——"

"Why, look here!" the Red Queen cried. "The dog would lose its temper, wouldn't it?"

"Perhaps it would," Alice replied cautiously.

"Then if the dog went away, its temper would remain!" the Queen exclaimed triumphantly.

Alice said, as gravely as she could, "They might go different ways." But she couldn't help thinking to herself, "What dreadful nonsense we *are* talking!"

"She can't do sums a *bit!*" the Queens said together, with great emphasis.

"Can *you* do sums?" Alice said, turning suddenly on the White Queen, for she didn't like being found fault with so much.

The Queen gasped and shut her eyes. "I can

do Addition," she said, " if you give me time—but I can't do Subtraction under *any* circumstances!"

"Of course you know your A B C?" said the Red Queen.

"To be sure I do," said Alice.

"So do I," the White Queen whispered: "we'll often say it over together, dear. And I'll tell you a secret—I can read words of one letter! Isn't *that* grand? However, don't be discouraged. You'll come to it in time."

Here the Red Queen began again. "Can you answer useful questions?" she said. "How is bread made?"

"I know that!" Alice cried eagerly. "You take some flour ——"

"Where do you pick the flower?" the White Queen asked. "In a garden, or in the hedges?"

"Well, it isn't *picked* at all," Alice explained: "it's *ground* ——"

"How many acres of ground?" said the White Queen. "You mustn't leave out so many things."

"Fan her head!" the Red Queen anxiously interrupted. "She'll be feverish after so much thinking." So they set to work and fanned her with bunches of leaves, till she had to beg them to leave off, it blew her hair about so.

" She's all right again now," said the Red Queen. " Do you know Languages? What's the French for fiddle-de-dee? "

" Fiddle-de-dee's not English," Alice replied gravely.

" Who ever said it was? " said the Red Queen.

Alice thought she saw a way out of the difficulty this time. " If you'll tell me what language ' fiddle-de-dee ' is, I'll tell you the French for it! " she exclaimed triumphantly.

But the Red Queen drew herself up rather stiffly, and said, " Queens never make bargains."

" I wish Queens never asked questions," Alice thought to herself.

" Don't let us quarrel," the White Queen said, in an anxious tone. " What is the cause of lightning? "

" The cause of lightning," Alice said, very decidedly, for she felt quite certain about this, " is the thunder—no, no! " she hastily corrected herself. " I meant the other way."

" It's too late to correct it," said the Red Queen: " when you've once said a thing, that fixes it, and you must take the consequences."

" Which reminds me," the White Queen said, looking down and nervously clasping and unclasping her hands, " we had *such* a thunderstorm last

Tuesday—I mean one of the last set of Tuesdays, you know."

Alice was puzzled. " In *our* country," she remarked, " there's only one day at a time."

The Red Queen said, " That's a poor, thin way of doing things. Now *here,* we mostly have days and nights two or three at a time, and sometimes in the winter we take as many as five nights together—for warmth, you know."

" Are five nights warmer than one night, then? " Alice ventured to ask.

" Five times as warm, of course."

" But they should be five times as *cold,* by the same rule ——"

" Just so! " cried the Red Queen. " Five times as warm, *and* five times as cold—just as I'm five times as rich as you are, *and* five times as clever! "

Alice sighed and gave it up. " It's exactly like a riddle with no answer," she thought.

" Humpty Dumpty saw it, too," the White Queen went on in a low voice, more as if she were talking to herself. " He came to the door with a corkscrew in his hand ——"

" What did he want? " said the Red Queen.

" He said he *would* come in," the White Queen went on, " because he was looking for a hippopotamus.  Now, as it happened there wasn't such a thing in the house that morning."

" Is there generally?" Alice asked in an astonished tone.

" Well, only on Thursdays," said the Queen.

" I know what he came for," said Alice.  " He wanted to punish the fish, because ——"

Here the White Queen began again.  " It was *such* a thunderstorm, you can't think!" (" She never could, you know," said the Red Queen.) " And part of the roof came off, and ever so much thunder got in—and it went rolling round the room in great lumps—and knocking over the tables and things—till I was so frightened, I couldn't remember my own name!"

Alice thought to herself, " I never should *try* to remember my name in the middle of an accident! Where would be the use of it?" but she did not say this aloud, for fear of hurting the poor Queen's feelings.

" Your Majesty must excuse her," the Red Queen said to Alice, taking one of the White Queen's hands in her own, and gently stroking it; " she means well, but she can't help saying foolish things, as a general rule."

The White Queen looked timidly at Alice, who

felt she *ought* to say something kind, but really couldn't think of anything at the moment.

" She never was really well brought up," the Red Queen went on; " but it's amazing how good-tempered she is! Pat her on the head, and see how pleased she'll be! " But this was more than Alice had courage to do.

" A little kindness—and putting her hair in papers—would do wonders with her ——"

The White Queen gave a deep sigh, and laid her head on Alice's shoulder. " I *am* so sleepy! " she moaned.

" She's tired, poor thing! " said the Red Queen. " Smooth her hair—lend her your nightcap—and sing her a soothing lullaby."

" I haven't got a nightcap with me," said Alice, as she tried to obey the first direction; " and I don't know any soothing lullabies."

" I must do it myself, then," said the Red Queen, and she began:

" Hush-aby, lady, in Alice's lap!
　　Till the feast's ready, we've time for a nap:
　When the feast's over, we'll go to the ball—
　　Red Queen, and White Queen, and Alice, and all!

" And now you know the words," she added, as she put her head down on Alice's other shoulder,

" just sing it through to *me*. I'm getting sleepy, and snoring loud."

" What *am* I to do? " exclaimed Alice, looking about in great perplexity, as first one round head, and then the other rolled down from her shoulder, and lay like a heavy lump in her lap.   " I don't think it *ever* happened before, that any one had to take care of two Queens asleep at once!   No, not in all the history of England—it couldn't, you know, because there never was more than one Queen at a time.   Do wake up, you heavy things! " she went on in an impatient tone; but there was no answer but a gentle snoring.

The snoring got more distinct every minute, and sounded more like a tune: at last she could even make out words and she listened so eagerly that when the two great heads suddenly vanished from her lap, she hardly missed them.

She was standing before an arched doorway over which were the words QUEEN ALICE in large letters, and on each side of the arch there was a bell handle: one marked " Visitors' Bell " and the other " Servants' Bell."

" I'll wait till the song's over," thought Alice, " and then I'll ring the—the—*which* bell must I ring? " she went on, very much puzzled by the names.   " I'm not a visitor, and I'm not a servant.

There *ought* to be one marked ' Queen,' you know ——"

Just then the door opened a little way, and a creature with a long beak put its head out for a moment and said, " No admittance till the week after next! " and shut the door again with a bang.

Alice knocked and rang in vain for a long time, but at last a very old Frog, who was sitting under a tree, got up and hobbled slowly toward her; he was dressed in bright yellow, and had enormous boots on.

" What is it now? " the Frog said in a deep hoarse whisper.

Alice turned round, ready to find fault with anybody.  " Where's the servant whose business it is to answer the door? " she began angrily.

" Which door? " said the Frog.

Alice almost stamped with irritation at the slow drawls in which he spoke.  " This door, of course! "

The Frog looked at the door with his large, dull eyes for a minute; then he went nearer and rubbed it with his thumb, as if he were trying whether the paint would come off, then he looked at Alice.

" To answer the door? " he said.  " What's it been asking of? "  He was so hoarse that Alice could scarcely hear him.

" I don't know what you mean," she said.

" I speaks English, doesn't I? " the Frog went on. " Or are you deaf? What did it ask you? "

" Nothing! " Alice said impatiently. " I've been knocking at it! "

" Shouldn't do that—shouldn't do that," the Frog muttered. " Wexes it, you know." Then he went up and gave the door a kick with one of his great feet. " You let it alone," he panted out, as he hobbled back to his tree, " and it'll let you alone, you know."

At this moment the door was flung open, and a shrill voice was heard singing:

" To the Looking-Glass world it was Alice that said,
  ' I've a sceptre in hand, I've a crown on my head;
  Let the Looking-Glass creatures, whatever they be,
  Come and dine with the Red Queen, the White Queen,
    and me!' "

Then followed a confused noise of cheering, and Alice thought to herself, " Thirty times three makes ninety. I wonder if any one's counting? " In a minute there was silence again, and the same shrill voice sang another verse:

" ' Oh, Looking-Glass creatures,' quoth Alice, ' draw near!
  'Tis an honor to see me, a favor to hear;
  'Tis a privilege high to have dinner and tea
  Along with the Red Queen, the White Queen, and
    me!' "

Then came the chorus again:

" Then fill up the glasses with treacles and ink,
  Or anything else that is pleasant to drink;
  Mix sand with the cider, and wool with the wine—
  And welcome Queen Alice with ninety-times-nine!"

" Ninety times nine!" Alice repeated in despair.
" Oh, that'll never be done! I'd better go in at
once," and in she went, and there was a dead silence
the moment she appeared.

Alice glanced nervously along the table, as she
walked up the large hall, and noticed that there
were about fifty guests of all kinds; some were animals, some birds, and there were even a few flowers
among them. " I'm glad they've come without
waiting to be asked," she thought; " I should never
have known who were the right people to invite!"

There were three chairs at the head of the table;
the Red and the White Queens had already taken
two of them, but the middle one was empty. Alice
sat down in it, rather uncomfortable at the silence,
and longing for some one to speak.

At last the Red Queen began. " You've missed
the soup and fish," she said. " Put on the joint."
And the waiters set a leg of mutton before Alice,
who looked at it rather anxiously, as she never had
to carve a joint before.

" You look a little shy; let me introduce you to

that leg of mutton," said the Red Queen. " Alice
—Mutton; Mutton—Alice." The leg of mutton
got up in the dish and made a little bow to Alice;
and Alice returned the bow, not knowing whether
to be frightened or amused.

" May I give you a slice?" she said, taking up
the knife and fork, and looking from one Queen to
the other.

" Certainly not," the Red Queen said, very decidedly; " it isn't etiquette to cut any one you've
been introduced to. Remove the joint!" And the
waiters carried it off, and brought a large plum-
pudding in its place.

" I won't be introduced to the pudding, please,"
Alice said rather hastily, " or we shall get no dinner at all. May I give you some?"

But the Red Queen looked sulky, and growled,
" Pudding—Alice; Alice—Pudding. Remove the
pudding!" and the waiters took it away so quickly
that Alice couldn't return its bow.

However, she didn't see why the Red Queen
should be the only one to give orders, so, as an
experiment, she called out, " Waiter! Bring back
the pudding!" and there it was again in a moment,
like a conjuring-trick! It was so large that she
couldn't help feeling a little shy with it, as she had
been with the mutton; however, she conquered her

shyness by a great effort, and cut a slice and handed
it to the Red Queen.

" What impertinence! " said the Pudding. " I
wonder how you'd like it, if I were to cut a slice out
of *you,* you creature! "

It spoke in a thick, suety sort of a voice, and
Alice hadn't a word to say in reply; she could only
sit and look at it and gasp.

" Make a remark," said the Red Queen; " it's
ridiculous to leave all the conversation to the pudding! "

" Do you know, I've had such a quantity of
poetry repeated to me to-day," Alice began, a little
frightened at finding that, the moment she opened
her lips, there was dead silence, and all eyes were
fixed upon her; " and it's a very curious thing, I
think—every poem was about fishes in some way.
Do you know why they're so fond of fishes, all about
here? "

She spoke to the Red Queen, whose answer was
a little wide of the mark. " As to fishes," she said,
very slowly and solemnly, putting her mouth close
to Alice's ear, " her White Majesty knows a lovely
riddle—all in poetry—all about fishes. Shall she
repeat it? "

" Her Red Majesty's very kind to mention it,"
the White Queen murmured into Alice's other ear,

in a voice like the cooing of a pigeon. " It would be *such* a treat! May I? "

" Please do," Alice said, very politely.

The White Queen laughed with delight, and stroked Alice's cheek. Then she began:

> " ' First, the fish must be caught.'
> That is easy: a baby, I think, could have caught it.
>     ' Next, the fish must be bought.'
> That is easy: a penny, I think, would have bought it.
>     ' Now cook me the fish! '
> That is easy, and will not take more than a minute.
>     ' Let it lie in a dish! '
> That is easy, because it already is in it.

> " ' Bring it here! Let me sup! '
> It is easy, to set such a dish on the table.
>     ' Take the dish-cover up! '
> Ah, that is so hard that I fear I'm unable!
>     For it holds it like glue—
> Holds the lid to the dish, while it lies in the middle:
>     Which is easiest to do,
> Un-dish-cover the fish, or dishcover the riddle? "

" Take a minute to think about it, and then guess," said the Red Queen. " Meanwhile, we'll drink your health—Queen Alice's health! " she screamed at the top of her voice, and all the guests began drinking it directly, and very queerly they managed it; some of them put their glasses upon their heads like extinguishers, and drank all that trickled down their faces—others upset the decanters, and drank the wine as it ran off the edges of the table—and three of them (who looked like kangaroos) scrambled into the dish of roast mutton, and began eagerly lapping up the gravy, "Just like pigs in a trough!" thought Alice.

"You ought to return thanks in a neat speech," the Red Queen said, frowning at Alice as she spoke.

"We must support you, you know," the White Queen whispered, as Alice got up to do it, very obediently, but a little frightened.

"Thank you very much," she whispered in reply, "but I can do quite well without."

"That wouldn't be at all the thing," the Red Queen said very decidedly; so Alice tried to submit to it with a good grace.

("And they *did* push so!" she said afterwards, when she was telling her sister the history of the feast. "You would have thought they wanted to squeeze me flat!") In fact it was rather difficult for her to keep in her place while she made her speech; the two Queens pushed her so, one on each side, that they nearly lifted her up into the air. "I rise to return thanks ——" Alice began; and she really *did* rise as she spoke, several inches; but she got hold of the edge of the table, and managed to pull herself down again.

" Take care of yourself! " screamed the White Queen, seizing Alice's hair with both hands. " Something's going to happen! "

And then (as Alice afterwards described it) all sorts of things happened in a moment. The candles all grew up to the ceiling, looking something like a bed of rushes with fireworks at the top. As to the bottles, they each took a pair of plates, which they hastily fitted on as wings, and so, with forks for legs, went fluttering about in all directions; " and very like birds they look," Alice thought to herself, as well as she could in the dreadful confusion that was beginning.

At this moment she heard a hoarse laugh at her side, and turned to see what was the matter with the White Queen, but instead of the Queen there was the leg of mutton sitting in the chair. " Here I am! " cried a voice from the soup-tureen, and Alice turned again, just in time to see the Queen's broad, good-natured face grinning at her for a moment over the edge of the tureen, before she disappeared into the soup.

There was not a moment to be lost. Already several of the guests were lying down in the dishes, and the soup-ladle was walking up the table towards Alice's chair, and beckoning to her impatiently to get out of its way.

" I can't stand this any longer!" she cried as she jumped up and seized the table-cloth with both hands; one good pull, and plates, dishes, guests, and candles came crashing down together in a heap on the floor.

# THE STRIKE

OLIVER HERFORD

ONE Mr. William Thingum Tite,
  His young wife's patience sorely tried;
She called her boy, as well she might,
  UNTIDINESS PERSONIFIED.

Whene'er he went to bed at night,
  He never put his things away,
But tossed his clothes to left or right,
  And where they fell he let them stay.

Now, worms are not the only folk
  That, when exasperated, turn.
Clothes, too, will turn (that's not a joke),
  As from this narrative you'll learn.

One night, when Mr. William lay
  Wrapped in the arms of Morpheus,
His clothes a meeting held, that they
  Their sad condition might discuss.

The Roll Call first of all was read,
  And when 'twas found that all were there,
Since he came nearest to the head,
  To Derby Hat they gave the chair.

" My Fellow Garments! " he began,
　　When every one at last was still,
" Let us put down the tyrant man! "
　　As with one voice they cried, " We will! "

" He calls himself Creation's Lord,
　　But were it not for me and you,
What would he do? "　With one accord
　　The meeting cried, " What could he do? "

" How could he go to ball or hop,
　　Or even walk the avenues? "
" Why, but for us he'd have to stop
　　At home, of course! " exclaimed the Shoes.

" Supposing, on the street, perhaps,
　　He met a lady that he knew—
How could he bow? "　The Hats and Caps
　　Shouted in unison, " That's true! "

" How could he even offer
　　His hand in saying, ' How d'ye do '?
You know to whom I now refer! "
　　" We do! " exclaimed the Gloves.　" We do! "

" And what is more, if we were not
　　Good Form," concluded Derby Hat,
" How ever from the common lot
　　Could he be told?　Now tell me that! "

A Resolution then, proposed
  By Oxford Shoe, and seconded
By White Cravat (no one opposed),
  Was passed—and this is how it read:

Whereas, one William Thingum Tite,
  Has shown himself for clothes unfit,
Whereas, we, Undersigned, this night
  Are painfully aware of it;

Whereas, said William never pays
  Us the attention that we like;
Resolved, unless he mend his ways,
  We, Undersigned, his clothes, will strike!

The Resolution being framed,
  And signed and sealed that very night,
A deputation then was named
  To wait on William Thingum Tite.

When William rose next day he wore
  A somewhat sad and thoughtful air.
Picking his clothes from off the floor,
  He smoothed them out with greatest care.

You would not know young William Tite
  If now he chanced to meet your eye;
He is a vision of delight;
  He keeps a valet,—that is why.

# A HOPELESS CASE

OLIVER HERFORD

HER sisters shunned her, half in fear
    And half in pity. " 'Tis too bad
She is not made as we—poor dear! "
    (Four leaves instead of Three she had.)

Said Doctor Bee: " Her case is rare
    And due to Influence prenatal.
To amputate I would not dare,
    The operation might be fatal.

" With Rest and Care and Simple Food
    She may outlive both you and me;
A change of scene might do her good."
    (One bag of Honey was his fee.)

" Take me! take me! " the clovers cry,
    To a maid bending wistful-eyed.
With gentle hand she puts them by,
    Till all but one are passed aside.

Before her sisters' wondering eyes
    Her leaves with kisses are told over.
" At last! at last! " the maiden cries,
    " I've found you, little Four-leaved clover."

# THE TOWER OF LONDON

## CHARLES FARRAR BROWNE
### (*Artemus Ward*)

" MR. PUNCH, MY DEAR SIR: I skurcely need inform you that your excellent Tower is very pop'lar with peple from the agricultooral districks, and it was chiefly them class which I found waitin at the gates the other mornin.

" I saw at once that the Tower was established on a firm basis. In the entire history of firm basisis I don't find a basis more firmer than this one.

" ' You have no Tower in America? ' said a man in the crowd, who had somehow detected my denomination.

" ' Alars! no,' I answered; ' we boste of our enterprise and improovements, and yit we are devoid of a Tower. America, oh my onhappy country! thou hast not got no Tower! It's a sweet Boon.'

" The gates was opened after a while, and we all purchist tickets and went into a waitin-room.

" ' My frens,' said a pale-faced little man, in black close, ' this is a sad day.'

" ' Inasmuch as to how? ' I said.

142

" ' I mean it is sad to think that so many peple have been killed within these gloomy walls. My frens, let us drop a tear!'

" ' No,' I said, ' you must excuse me. Others may drop one if they feel like it; but as for me, I decline. The early managers of this institootion were a bad lot, and their crimes were trooly orful; but I can't sob for those who died four or five hundred years ago. If they was my own relations I couldn't. It's absurd to shed sobs over things which occurd durin the rain of Henry the Three. Let us be cheerful,' I continued. ' Look at the festiv Warders, in their red flannel jackets. They are cheerful, and why should it not be thusly with us?'

" A Warder now took us in charge, and showed us the Trater's Gate, the armers, and things. The Trater's Gate is wide enuff to admit about twenty traters abrest, I should jedge; but beyond this, I couldn't see that it was superior to gates in gen'ral.

" Traters, I will here remark, are a onfortnit class of peple. If they wasn't, they wouldn't be traters. They conspire to bust up a country—they fail, and they're traters. They bust her, and they become statesmen and heroes.

" Take the case of Gloster, afterwards Old Dick the Three, who may be seen at the Tower, on horseback, in a heavy tin overcoat—take Mr. Gloster's case. Mr. G. was a conspirator of the basist dye, and if he'd failed, he would have been hung on a sour apple tree. But Mr. G. succeeded, and became great. He was slewd by Col. Richmond, but he lives in histry, and his equestrian figger may be seen daily for a sixpence, in conjunction with other em'nent persons, and no extra for the Warder's able and bootiful lectur.

"There's one king in the room who is mounted onto a foamin steed, his right hand graspin a barber's pole. I didn't learn his name.

"The room where the daggers and pistils and other weppins is kept is interestin. Among this collection of choice cutlery I notist the bow and arrer which those hot-heded old chaps used to conduct battles with. It is quite like the bow and arrer used at this day by certain tribes of American Injuns, and they shoot 'em off with such a excellent precision that I almost sigh'd to be a Injun, when I was in the Rocky Mountain regin. They are a pleasant lot them Injuns. Mr. Cooper and Dr. Catlin have told us of the red man's wonerful eloquence, and I found it so. Our party was stopt on the plains of Utah by a band of Shoshones, whose chief said, ' Brothers! the pale-face is welcome. Brothers! the sun is sinkin in the West, and Warrabucky-she will soon cease speakin. Brothers! the

poor red man belongs to a race which is fast be-
comin extink.' He then whooped in a shrill manner, stole all our blankets and whisky, and fled to
the primeval forest to conceal his emotions.

" I will remark here, while on the subjeck of
Injuns, that they are in the main a very shaky
set,  . . .  and when I hear philanthropists
bewailin the fack that every year ' carries the noble
red man nearer the settin sun,' I simply have to say
I'm glad of it, tho' it is rough on the settin sun.
They call you by the sweet name of Brother one
minit, and the next they scalp you with their
Thomashawks. But I wander. Let us return to
the Tower.

" At one end of the room where the weppins is
kept, is a wax figger of Queen Elizabeth, mounted
on a fiery stuffed hoss, whose glass eye flashes with
pride, and whose red morocker nostril dilates
hawtily, as if conscious of the royal burden he bears.
I have associated Elizabeth with the Spanish
Armady.

" The Warder shows us some instrooments of
tortur, such as thumbscrews, throat-collars, etc.,
statin that these was conkered from the Spanish
Armady, and addin what a crooil peple the
Spaniards was in them days—which elissited from
a bright-eyed little girl of about twelve summers

the remark that she tho't it *was* rich to talk about the crooilty of the Spaniards usin thumbscrews when we was in a Tower where so many poor peple's heads had been cut off. This made the Warder stammer and turn red.

"The sad-lookin man, who had wanted us to drop a tear afore we started to go round, said to me, in the Beauchamp Tower, where the poor prisoners writ their onhappy names on the cold walls, ' This is a sad sight.'

"Indeed, he was quite right. Tho' so long ago all these drefful things happened, I was very glad to git away from this gloomy room, and go where the rich and sparklin Crown Jewils is kept. I was so pleased with the Queen's Crown, that it occurd to me what a agree'ble surprise it would be to send a sim'lar one home to my wife; and I asked the Warder what was the vally of a good, well-constructed Crown like that. He told me, but on cypherin up with a pencil the amount of funs I have in the Jint Stock Bank, I conclooded I'd send her a genteel silver watch instid.

"And so I left the Tower. It is a solid and commandin edifis, but I deny that it is cheerful. I bid it adoo without a pang.

"Respectably, &c.

"ARTEMUS WARD."

# AFTER MARY HOWITT
### (*The Lobster Quadrille*)

## CHARLES LUTWIDGE DODGSON
### (*Lewis Carroll*)

" WILL you walk a little faster? " said a whiting to
    a snail.
" There's a porpoise close behind us, and he's tread-
    ing on my tail.
See how eagerly the lobsters and the turtles all
    advance!
They are waiting on the shingle—will you come
    and join the dance?
Will you, won't you, will you, won't you, will
    you join the dance?
Will you, won't you, will you, won't you, won't
    you join the dance?

" You can really have no notion how delightful it
    will be
When they take us up and throw us, with the
    lobsters, out to sea! "
But the snail replied, " Too far, too far! " and
    gave a look askance—

Said he thanked the whiting kindly, but he would
   not join the dance.

Would not, could not, would not, could not,
   would not join the dance.

Would not, could not, would not, could not,
   would not join the dance.

" What matters it how far we go? " his scaly friend
   replied,

" There is another shore, you know, upon the other
   side.

The farther off from England the nearer is to
   France—

Then turn not pale, beloved snail, but come and
   join the dance.

Will you, won't you, will you, won't you, will
   you join the dance?

Will you, won't you, will you, won't you, won't
   you join the dance? "

# AUNT TABITHA

### Oliver Wendell Holmes

Whatever I do, and whatever I say,
Aunt Tabitha tells me that isn't the way;
When *she* was a girl (forty summers ago)
Aunt Tabitha tells me they never did so.

Dear aunt! If I only would take her advice!
But I like my own way, and I find it *so* nice!
And besides, I forget hálf the things I am told;
But they all will come back to me—when I am
old.

If a youth passes by, it may happen, no doubt,
He may chance to look in as I chance to look out;
*She* would never endure an impertinent stare,—
It is *horrid,* she says, and I mustn't sit there.

A walk in the moonlight has pleasures, I own,
But it isn't quite safe to be walking alone;
So I take a lad's arm,—just for safety, you
know,—
But Aunt Tabitha tells me *they* didn't do so.

How wicked we are, and how good they were
    then!
They kept at arm's length those detestable men;
What an era of virtue she lived in!—But stay—
Were the *men* all such rogues in Aunt Tabitha's
    day!

If the men *were* so wicked, I'll ask my papa
How he dared to propose to my darling mamma;
Was he like the rest of them?  Goodness!  Who
    knows?
And what shall *I* say, if a wretch should propose?

I am thinking if Aunt knew so little of sin,
What a wonder Aunt Tabitha's aunt must have
    been!
And her grand-aunt—it scares me—how shock-
    ingly sad
That we girls of to-day are so frightfully bad!

A martyr will save us, and nothing else can;
Let me perish—to rescue some wretched young
    man!
Though when to the altar a victim I go,
Aunt Tabitha'll tell me *she* never did so!

# LIMERICKS

## Edward Lear

There was an old man of Thermopylæ,
Who never did anything properly;
   But they said: " If you choose
   To boil eggs in your shoes,
You cannot remain in Thermopylæ."

There was an old man who said, " Hush!
I perceive a young bird in this bush!"
   When they said, " Is it small?"
   He replied, " Not at all;
It is four times as big as the bush!"

There was a young lady of Niger
Who smiled as she rode on a Tiger;
   They came back from the ride
   With the lady inside,
And the smile on the face of the Tiger.
                *—Anonymous.*

There was a young maid who said, " Why
Can't I look in my ear with my eye?
   If I give my mind to it,
   I'm sure I can do it,
You never can tell till you try."
                *—Anonymous.*

# KING HENRY IV

## WILLIAM SHAKESPEARE

ACT I. Extract from Scene II. London. An apartment of the Prince.

Enter the Prince of Wales, Falstaff and Poins.

*Poins.* But, my lads, my lads, to-morrow morning, by four o'clock early at Gadshill! there are pilgrims going to Canterbury with rich offerings, and traders riding to London with fat purses: I have visards for you all, you have horses for yourselves: Gadshill lies to-night in Rochester: I have bespoke supper to-morrow night in Eastcheap: we may do it as secure as sleep. If you will go, I will stuff your purses full of crowns; if you will not, tarry at home and be hanged.

*Fal.* Hear ye, Edward; if I tarry at home and go not, I'll hang you for going.

*Poins.* You will, chops?

*Fal.* Hal, wilt thou make one?

*P. Hen.* Who, I rob? I a thief? not I, my faith.

*Fal.* There's neither honesty, manhood, nor good fellowship in thee nor thou camest not of the blood royal, if thou darest not stand for ten shillings.

*P. Hen.* Well, then, once in my days I'll be a madcap.

*Fal.* Why, that's well said.

*P. Hen.* Well, come what will, I'll tarry at home.

*Fal.* I'll be a traitor, then, when thou art king.

*P. Hen.* I care not.

*Poins.* Sir John, I prithee, leave the prince and me alone: I will lay him down such reasons for this adventure, that he shall go.

*Fal.* Well, God give thee the spirit of persuasion, and him the ears of profiting, that what thou speakest may move, and what he hears may be believed, that the true prince may (for recreation sake) prove a false thief; for the poor abuses of the time want countenance. Farewell; you shall find me in Eastcheap.

*P. Hen.* Farewell, thou latter spring! Farewell, All-hallown summer!

*Poins.* Now, my good sweet honey lord, ride with us alone. Falstaff, Bardolph, Peto, and Gadshill shall rob those men that we have already waylaid; yourself and I will not be there; and when they have the booty, if you and I do not rob them, cut this head off from my shoulders.

*P. Hen.* But how shall we part with them in setting forth?

*Poins.* Why, we will set forth before or after them, and appoint them a place of meeting, wherein it is our pleasure to fail; and then will they adventure upon the exploit themselves; which they have no sooner achieved, but we'll set upon them.

*P. Hen.* Ay, but 'tis like that they will know us by our horses, by our habits, and by every other appointment, to be ourselves.

*Poins.* Tut! our horses they shall not see,—I'll tie them in the wood; our visards we will change, after we leave them: and, sirrah, I have cases of buckram for the nonce, to unmask our noted outward garments.

*P. Hen.* But I doubt they will be too hard for us.

*Poins.* Well, for two of them, I know them to be as truebred cowards as ever turned back; and for the third, if he fight longer than he sees reason, I'll forswear arms. The virtue of this jest will be, the incomprehensible lies that this same fat rogue will tell, when we meet at supper; how thirty, at least, he fought with; what wards, what blows, what extremities he endured; and, in the reproof of this, lies the jest.

*P. Hen.* Well, I'll go with thee; provide us all

things necessary and meet me to-morrow night in Eastcheap; there I'll sup. Farewell.

*Poins.* Farewell, my lord.

Extract from Act II, Scene IV. The Buckram-Men Scene.

Enter the Prince, Falstaff, Gadshill, Poins, Peto, and Francis bearing wine.

*Poins.* Welcome, Jack. Where hast thou been?

*Fal.* A plague of all cowards, I say, and a vengeance, too! marry, and amen. Give me a cup of sack, boy. Ere I lead this life long, I'll sew nether-stocks, and mend them, and foot them too. A plague of all cowards! Give me a cup of sack, rogue. Is there no virtue extant?

*P. Hen.* Didst thou never see Titan kiss a dish of butter? Pitiful-hearted Titan, that melted at the sweet tale of the Sun's! If thou didst, then behold that compound.

*Fal.* You rogue, here's lime in this sack too. There is nothing but roguery to be found in villainous man. Yet a coward is worse than a cup of sack with lime in it; a villainous coward—Go thy way, old Jack; die when thou wilt, if manhood, good manhood, be not forgot upon the face of the earth, then I am a herring. There live not three good men unhanged in England; and one of them is fat, and grows old; God help the while! a bad world, I say! I would I were a weaver; I could sing psalms of anything: a plague of all cowards, I say still.

*P. Hen.* How now, woolsack? what mutter you?

*Fal.* A king's son? If I do not beat thee out of thy kingdom with a dagger of lath, and drive all thy subjects afore thee like a flock of wild geese, I'll never wear hair on my face more. You, Prince of Wales!

*P. Hen.* Why, what's the matter?

*Fal.* Are you not a coward? Answer me to that; and Poins there?

*Poins.* Call me coward, I'll stab thee!

*Fal.* I call thee coward! I'll see thee hanged ere I call thee coward; but I would give a thousand pound, I could run as fast as thou canst. You are straight enough in the shoulders, you care not who sees your back. Call you that, lacking of your friends? A plague upon such backing! Give me them that will face me. Give me a cup of sack.

*P. Hen.* O villain! thy lips are scarce wiped since thou drunk'st last.

*Fal.* All's one for that. A plague of all cowards, still say I.

*P. Hen.* What's the matter?

*Fal.* What's the matter?  There be four of us here have ta'en a thousand pound this morning.

*P. Hen.* Where is it, Jack, where is it?

*Fal.* Where is it?  Taken from us it is; a hundred upon poor four of us.

*P. Hen.* What, a hundred, man?

*Fal.* I am a rogue, if I were not at half-sword with a dozen of them two hours together.  I have 'scaped by miracle.  I am eight times thrust through the doublet; four through the hose; my buckler cut through and through; my sword hacked like a hand-saw, *ecce signum*.  I never dealt better since I was a man; all would not do.  A plague of all cowards!  Let them speak, if they speak more or less than truth, they are villains, and the sons of darkness.

*P. Hen.* Speak, sirs, how was it?

*Gads.* We four set upon some dozen ——

*Fal.* Sixteen, at least, my lord.

*Gads.* And bound them.

*Peto.* No, no, they were not bound.

*Fal.* You rogue, they were bound, every man of them, or I am a Jew else a Ebrew Jew.

*Gads.* As we were sharing, some six or seven fresh men set upon us ——

*Fal.* And unbound the rest, and then come in the other.

*P. Hen.* What, fought ye with them all?

*Fal.* All? I know not what ye call all, but if I fought not with fifty of them, I am a bunch of radish: if there were not two or three and fifty upon poor old Jack, then I am no two-legged creature.

*Poins.* Pray God, you have not murdered some of them.

*Fal.* Nay, that's past praying for: I have peppered two of them: two, I am sure, I have paid: two rogues in buckram suits. I tell thee what, Hal, if I tell thee a lie, spit in my face, call me a horse. Thou knowest my old ward;—here I lay, and thus I bore my point. Four rogues in buckram let drive at me ——

*P. Hen.* What, four? thou said'st but two, even now.

*Fal.* Four, Hal, I told thee four.

*Poins.* Ay, ay, he said four.

*Fal.* These four came all a-front, and mainly thrust at me. I made me no more ado, but took all their seven points in my target, thus.

*P. Hen.* Seven? why there were but four, even now.

*Fal.* In buckram.

*Poins.* Ay, four, in buckram suits.

*Fal.* Seven, by these hilts, or I am a villain else.

*P. Hen.* Prithee, let him alone, we shall have more anon.

*Fal.* Dost thou hear me, Hal?

*P. Hen.* Ay, and mark thee too, Jack.

*Fal.* Do so, for it is worth the listening to. These nine in buckram, that I told thee of ——

*P. Hen.* So, two more already.

*Fal.* Their points being broken ——

*Poins.* Down fell their hose.

*Fal.* Began to give me ground. But I followed me close, came in foot and hand, and, with a thought, seven of the eleven I paid.

*P. Hen.* O monstrous! eleven buckram men grown out of two!

*Fal.* But, as the devil would have it, three mis-begotten knaves, in Kendal green, came at my back, and let drive at me;—for it was so dark, Hal, that thou could'st not see thy hand.

*P. Hen.* Why, how could'st thou know these men in Kendal green, when it was so dark thou could'st not see thy hand? Come tell us your reason. What sayest thou to this?

*Poins.* Come, your reason, Jack, your reason.

*Fal.* What, upon compulsion? No, were I at the strappado, or all the racks in the world, I would not tell you upon compulsion. Give you a reason on compulsion! If reasons were as plenty as blackberries I would give no man a reason upon compulsion, I ——

*P. Hen.* Well, breathe a while, and then to it again, and when thou hast tired thyself in base comparisons, hear me speak but this.

*Poins.* Mark, Jack.

*P. Hen.* We two saw you four set on four, you bound them, and were masters of their wealth. Mark now how plain a tale shall you put down. Then did we two set on you four, and, with a word, out-faced you from your prize, and have it; yea, and can show it to you here in the house, and, Falstaff, you ran, with as quick dexterity, and roared for mercy, and still ran and roared, as ever I heard a calf. What a slave art thou, to hack thy sword as thou hast done; and then say, it was in fight! What trick, what device, what starting-hole, canst thou now find out, to hide thee from this open and apparent shame?

*Poins.* Come, let's hear, Jack. What trick hast thou now?

*Fal.* By the Lord, I knew ye, as well as he who made ye. Why, hear ye, my masters. Was it for me to kill the heir apparent? Should I turn upon the true Prince? Why, thou knowest, I am as valiant as Hercules but beware instinct, the lion will not touch the true prince. Instinct is a great matter, I was a coward on instinct. I shall think the better of myself, and thee during my life; I, for a valiant lion, and thou for a true prince. But by the Lord, lads, I am glad you have the money. Hostess, clap to the doors; watch to-night, pray to-morrow. Gallants, lads, boys, hearts of gold, all the titles of good fellowship come to you! What shall we be merry? Shall we have a play extempore?

*P. Hen.* Content,—and the argument shall be thy running away.

*Fal.* Ah, no more of that, Hal, an thou lovest me.

# SEEIN' THINGS

### Eugene Field

I AIN'T afeard uv snakes, or toads, or bugs, or
  worms, or mice,
An' things 'at girls are skeered uv I think are awful
  nice!
I'm pretty brave, I guess: an' yet I hate to go to
  bed,
For, when I'm tucked up warm an' snug an' when
  my prayers are said,
Mother tells me, " Happy dreams!" and takes
  away the light,
An' leaves me lyin' all alone an' seein' things at
  night!

Sometimes they're in the corner, sometimes they're
  by the door,
Sometimes they're all a-standin' in the middle of
  the floor:
Sometimes they are a-sittin' down, sometimes
  they're walkin' round
So softly an' so creepylike they never make a
  sound!

Sometimes they are as black as ink, an' other times
    they're white—
But the color ain't no difference when you see
    things at night!

Once, when I licked a feller 'at had just moved
    on our street,
An' father sent me up to bed without a bite to eat,
I woke up in the dark an' saw things standin' in a
    row,
A-lookin' at me cross-eyed an' p'intin' at me—so!
Oh, my!  I wuz so skeered that time I never slep'
    a mite—
It's almost alluz when I'm bad I see things at
    night!

Lucky thing I ain't a girl, or I'd be skeered to
    death!
Bein' I'm a boy, I duck my head an' hold my
    breath:
An' I am, oh! *so* sorry I'm a naughty boy, an'
    then
I promise to be better an' I say my prayers again!
Gran'ma tells me that's the only way to make it
    right
When a feller has been wicked an' sees things at
    night!

An' so, when other naughty boys would coax me
  into sin,
I try to skwush the Tempter's voice 'at urges me
  within:
An' when they's pie for supper, or cakes 'at's big
  an' nice,
I want to—but I do not pass my plate f'r them
  things twice!
No, ruther let Starvation wipe me slowly out o'
  sight
Than I should keep a-livin' on an' seein' things at
  night!

# OLD CHUMS

## Alice Cary

Is that you, Jack?   Old boy, is it really you?
  I shouldn't have known you, but that I was told
You might be expected; pray, how do you do?
  But what under heaven has made you so old?

Your hair! why, you've only a little gray fuzz!
  And your beard's white! but that can be beauti-
      fully dyed;
And your legs aren't but just half as long as they
      was;
  And then—stars and garters! your vest is so
      wide!

Is this your hand?   Lord, how I envied you that
  In the time of your courting,—so soft and so
      small,
And now it is callous inside, and so fat,
  Well, you beat the very old deuce, that is all.

Turn round!   Let me look at you! isn't it odd,
  How strange in a few years a fellow's chum
      grows!

Your eye is shrunk up like a bean in a pod,
    And what are these lines branching out from
        your nose?

Your back has gone up and your shoulders gone
        down,
    And all the old roses are under the plow;
Why, Jack, if we'd happened to meet about town,
    I wouldn't have known you from Adam, I vow!

You've had trouble, have you?  I'm sorry; but,
        John,
    All trouble sits lightly at your time of life.
How's Billy, my namesake?  You don't say he's
        gone
    To the war, John, and that you have buried your
        wife?

Poor Katherine! so she has left you, ah me!
    I thought she would live to be fifty or more.
What is it you tell me?   She was fifty-three!
    Oh, no, Jack! she wasn't so much by a score!

Well, there's little Katy,—was that her name,
        John?
    She'll rule your house one of these days like a
        queen.
That baby! good Lord! is she married and gone?
    With a Jack ten years old! and a Katy fourteen!

Then I give it up!   Why, you're younger than I
  By ten or twelve years, and to think you've come
      back
A sober old graybeard, just ready to die!
  I don't understand how it is, do you, Jack?

I've got all my faculties yet, sound and bright;
  Slight failure my eyes are beginning to hint;
But still, with my spectacles on, and a light
  Betwixt them and the page, I can read any print.

My hearing is dull and my leg is more spare,
  Perhaps than it was when I beat you at ball;
My breath gives out, too, if I go up a stair,—
  But nothing worth mentioning, nothing at all!

My hair is just turning a little, you see,
  And lately I've put on a broader-brimmed hat
Than I wore at your wedding, but you will agree,
  Old fellow, I look all the better for that.

I'm sometimes a little rheumatic, 'tis true,
  And my nose isn't quite on a straight line, they
      say;
For all that, I don't think I have changed much,
      do you?
  And I don't feel a day older, Jack, not a day.

# WHY MR. DOG IS TAME

## Joel Chandler Harris

Uncle Remus paused and pulled a raveling from his shirt-sleeve, looking at the little boy meanwhile.

" I know very well you haven't forgotten the story," remarked the child, " for Grandmother says you never forget anything, especially the old-time tales."

" Well, suh, I speck she knows. She been knowin' me ev'ry sence she wuz a baby gal, an' mo' dan dat, she know right p'int blank what I'm a-thinkin' 'bout when she kin git her eye on me."

" And she says she never caught you tellin' a fib."

" Is she say dat? " Uncle Remus inquired with a broad grin. " Ef she did, I'm lots sharper dan I looks ter be, kaze many and many's de time when I been skeer'd white, thinkin' she done cotch me. Tooby sho', tooby sho'! "

" But what about the Dog, Uncle Remus? "

" What dog, honey? Oh, you'll hatter scuzen me—I'm lots older dan what I looks ter be. You mean de Dog what tuck up at Mr. Man's house.

168

Well, ol' Brer Dog wuz e'en about like he is deze days, scratchin' fer fleas, an' growlin' over his vittles stidder sayin' grace, an' berryin' de bones when he had one too many. He wuz des like he is now, 'ceppin' dat he wuz wil'. He galloped wid Brer Fox, an' loped wid Brer Wolf, an' cantered wid Brer Coon. He went all de gaits, an' he had dez ez good a time ez any un um, an' dez ez bad a time.

"Now, one day, some'rs 'twix' Monday mornin' an' Saddy night, he wuz settin' in de shade scratchin' hisse'f, an' he wuz tooken wid a spell er thinkin'. He'd des come thoo a mighty hard winter wid de yuther creeturs, an' he up an' say ter hisse'f dat ef he had ter do like dat one mo' season, it'd be de enn' er him an' his fambly. You could count his ribs, an' his hip-bones stuck out like de horns on a hat-rack.

"Whiles he wuz settin' dar, scratchin' an' studyin', an' studyin' an' scratchin', who should come meanderin' down de big road but ol' Brer Wolf; an' it 'uz ' Hello, Brer Dog! you look like you ain't seed de inside uv a smokehouse fer quite a whet. I ain't sayin' dat I got much fer ter brag on, kaze I ain't in no better fix dan what you is. De colder it gits, de skacer de vittles grows.' An' den he ax Brer Dog whar he gwine an' how soon he gwineter git dar. Brer Dog make answer dat it don't make no diffunce whar he go ef he don't fin' dinner ready.

"Brer Wolf 'low dat de way ter git dinner is ter make a fier, kaze 'tain't no use fer ter try ter eat ef dey don't do dat.   Ef dey don't git nothin' fer ter cook, dey'll have a place whar dey kin keep warm. Brer Dog say he see whar Brer Wolf is dead right, but whar dey gwine git a fier?   Brer Wolf say de quickest way is ter borry a chunk fum Mr. Man er his ol' 'oman.   But when it come ter sayin' who gwine atter it, dey bofe kinder hung back, kaze dey know'd dat Mr. Man had a walkin-cane what he kin p'int at anybody an' snap a cap on it an' blow der light right out.

"But bimeby, Brer Dog say'll go atter de chunk er fier, an' he ain't no mo' dan say dat, 'fo' off he put, an' he travel so peart, dat 'twan't long 'fo' he come ter Mr. Man's house.   When he got ter de gate he sot down an' done some mo' studyin', an' ef de gate had 'a' been shot, he'd 'a' turned right roun' an' went back like he come; but some er de chillun had been playin' out in de yard, an' dey lef' de gate open, an' so dar 'twuz.   Study ez he mought, he can't fin' no skuce fer gwine back widout de chunk fer fier.   An' in he went.

"Well, talk 'bout folks bein' 'umble; you ain't seed no 'umble-come-tumble twel you see Brer Dog

when he went in dat gate.   He ain't take time fer
ter look roun', he so skeer'd.   He hears hogs
a-gruntin' an' pigs a-squealin', he hear hens
a-cacklin' an' roosters crowin', but he ain't turn his
head.   He had sense 'nuff not ter go in de house
by de front way.   He went roun' de back way whar
de kitchen wuz, an' when he got dar he 'fraid ter go
any furder.   He went ter de do', he did, an' he
'fraid ter knock.   He hear chillun laughin' an'
playin' in dar, an' fer de fust time in all his born
days, he 'gun ter feel lonesome.

" Bimeby, some un open de do' an' den shot it
right quick.   But Brer Dog ain't see nobody; he 'uz
too 'umble-come-tumble fer dat.   He wuz lookin' at
de groun', an' wonderin' what 'uz gwinter happen
nex'.   It must 'a' been one er de chillun what open
de do', kaze 'twan't long 'fo' here come Mr. Man
wid de walkin-cane what had fier in it.   He come
ter de do', he did, an' he say, ' What you want
here?'   Brer Dog wuz too skeer'd fer ter talk; all
he kin do is ter des wag his tail.   Mr. Man, he 'low,
' You in de wrong house, an' you better go on whar
you got some business.'

" Brer Dog, he crouch down close ter de groun',
an' wag his tail.   Mr. Man, he look at 'im, an' he
ain't know whedder fer ter turn loose his gun er
not, but his ol' 'oman, she hear him talkin', an' she

come ter de do', an' see Brer Dog crouchin' dar,
'umbler dan de 'umblest, an' she say, ' Po' feller!
you ain't gwine ter hurt nobody, is you?' an' Brer
Dog 'low, ' No, ma'am, I ain't; I des come fer ter
borry a chunk er fier.' An' she say, ' What in de
name er goodness does you want wid fier? Is you
gwine ter burn us out' house an' home?' Brer
Dog 'low, ' No, ma'am! dat I ain't; I des wanter git
warm.' Den de 'oman say, ' I clean fergot 'bout
de col' wedder—come in de kitchen here an' warm
yo'se'f much ez you wanter.'

"Dat wuz mighty good news fer Brer Dog, an'
in he went. Dey wuz a nice big fier on de h'ath,
an' de chillun wuz settin' all roun' eatin' der dinner.
Dey make room fer Brer Dog, an' down he sot in
a warm cornder, an' 'twan't long 'fo' he wuz feelin'
right splimmy-splammy. But he wuz mighty
hongry. He sot dar, he did, an' watch de chillun
eatin' der ashcake an' buttermilk, an' his eyeballs
'ud foller eve'y mouffle dey e't. De 'oman, she
notice dis, an' she went ter de cubberd an' got a
piece er warm ashcake, an' put it down on de h'ath.

"Brer Dog ain't need no secon' invite—he des
gobble up de ashcake 'fo' you kin say Jack Robber-
son wid yo' mouf shot. He ain't had nigh nuff,
but he know'd better dan ter show what his ap-
petites wuz. He 'gun ter feel good, an' den he got

down on his hunkers, an' lay his head down on his fo' paws, an' make like he gwine ter sleep. Atter 'while, he smell Brer Wolf, an' he raise his head an' look todes de do'. Mr. Man he tuck notice, an' he say he b'lieve dey's some un sneakin' roun'. Brer Dog raise his head, an' snuff todes de do', an' growl ter hisse'f. So Mr. Man tuck down his gun fum over de fierplace, an' went out. De fust thing he see when he git out in de yard wuz Brer Wolf runnin' out de gate, an' he up wid his gun—bang!— an' he hear Brer Wolf holler. All he got wuz a han'ful er ha'r, but he come mighty nigh gittin' de whole hide.

" Well, atter dat, Mr. Man fin' out dat Brer Dog could do 'im a heap er good, fus' one way an' den an'er. He could head de cows off when dey make a break thoo de woods, he could take keer er de sheep, an' he could warn Mr. Man when some er de yuther creeturs wuz prowlin' roun'. An' den he wuz some comp'ny when Mr. Man went huntin'. He could trail de game, an' he could fin' his way home fum anywheres; an' he could play wid de chillun des like he wuz one un um.

" 'Twan't long 'fo' he got fat, an' one day when he wuz amblin' in de woods, he meet up wid Brer Wolf. He howdied at 'im, he did, but Brer Wolf won't skacely look at 'im. Atter 'while he say,

'Brer Dog, whyn't you come back dat day when
you went atter fier?' Brer Dog p'int ter de collar
on his neck. He 'low, 'You see dis? Well, it'll
tell you lots better dan what I kin.' Brer Wolf
say, 'You mighty fat. Why can't I come dar an'
do like you does?' Brer Dog 'low, 'Dey ain't
nothin' fer ter hinder you.'

"So de next mornin', bright an' early, Brer Wolf
knock at Mr. Man's do'. Mr. Man peep out an'
see who 'tis, an' tuck down his gun an' went out.
Brer Wolf try ter be perlite, an' he smile. But
when he smile he show'd all his tushes, an' dis kinder
skeer Mr. Man. He say, 'What you doin'
sneakin' roun' here?' Brer Wolf try ter be mo'
perliter dan ever, an' he grin fum year ter year.
Dis show all his tushes, an' Mr. Man lammed
a-loose at 'im. An' dat 'uz de las' time dat Brer
Wolf ever try ter live wid Mr. Man, an' fum dat
time on down ter dis day, it 'uz war 'twix' Brer
Wolf an' Brer Dog."

# JENNY WREN

## Mother Goose

'Twas on a merry time, when Jenny Wren was
   young,
So neatly as she danced, and so sweetly as she
   sung,—

Robin Redbreast lost his heart—he was a gallant
   bird;
He doffed his hat to Jenny, and thus to her he
   said:—

" My dearest Jenny Wren, if you will but be mine,
   You shall dine on cherry-pie, and drink nice
   currant-wine.

" I'll dress you like a Goldfinch, or like a peacock
   gay;
   So if you'll have me, Jenny, let us appoint the
   day."

Jenny blushed behind her fan, and thus declared
   her mind,
" Then let it be to-morrow, Bob; I take your offer
   kind.

" Cherry-pie is very good; so is currant-wine;
   But I will wear my brown gown, and never dress
   too fine."

Robin rose up early, at the break of day;
He flew to Jenny Wren's house, to sing a
roundelay.

He met the Cock and Hen, and bade the Cock
declare,
This was his wedding-day with Jenny Wren the
fair.

The Cock then blew his horn, to let the neighbors
know
This was Robin's wedding-day, and they might
see the show.

And first came Parson Rook, with his spectacles
and band;
And one of Mother Goose's books he held within
his hand.

Then followed him the Lark, for he could sweetly
sing;
And he was to be clerk at Cock Robin's wedding.

He sung of Robin's love for little Jenny Wren;
And when he came unto the end, then he began
again.

The Bullfinch walked by Robin and thus to him
did say,
" Pray, mark, friend Robin Redbreast, that Goldfinch dressed so gay;—

" What though her gay apparel becomes her very
well;
Yet Jenny's modest dress and look must bear
away the bell! "

Then came the bride and bridegroom; quite
plainly was she dressed;
And blushed so much, her cheeks were as red as
Robin's breast.

But Robin cheered her up; " My pretty Jen,"
said he,
" We're going to be married, and happy we shall
be."

The Goldfinch came on next, to give away the
bride;
The Linnet, being bridesmaid, walked by Jenny's
side.

And as she was a-walking, said, "Upon my
   word,
I think that your Cock Robin is a very pretty
   bird."


" And will you have her, Robin, to be your wedded
   wife? "
" Yes, I will," says Robin, " and love her all my
   life."


" And you will have him, Jenny, your husband now
   to be? "
" Yes, I will," says Jenny, " and love him
   heartily."


The Blackbird and the Thrush, and charming
   Nightingale,
Whose sweet " jug " sweetly echoes through
   every grove and dale;—


The Sparrow and Tomtit, and many more were
   there;
All came to see the wedding of Jenny Wren the
   fair.

" Oh, then," says Parson Rook, " who gives this
maid away? "

" I do," says the Goldfinch, " and her fortune I
will pay;—

" Here's a bag of grain of many sorts, and other
things beside;
Now happy be the bridegroom, and happy be the
bride! "

Then on her finger fair, Cock Robin put the ring;
" You're married now," says Parson Rook; while
the Lark aloud did sing,—

" Happy be the bridegroom, and happy be the
bride!
And may not man, nor bird, nor beast, this happy
pair divide."

The birds were asked to dine; not Jenny's friends
alone,
But every pretty songster that had Cock Robin
known.

They had a cherry-pie, besides some currant-
wine,
And every guest brought something, that sump-
tuous they might dine.

Now they all sat or stood, to eat and to drink;
And every one said what he happened to think.

They each took a bumper, and drank to the pair;
Cock Robin the bridegroom, and Jenny Wren
    the fair.

The dinner things removed, they all began to
    sing;
And soon they made the place near a mile around
    to ring.

The concert it was fine; and every bird tried
Who best should sing for Robin, and Jenny
    Wren the bride.

When in came the Cuckoo, and made a great
    rout;
He caught hold of Jenny, and pulled her about.

Cock Robin was angry, and so was the Sparrow,
Who fetched in a hurry his bow and his arrow.

His aim then he took, but he took it not right;
His skill was not good, or he shot in a fright;

For the Cuckoo he missed,—but Cock Robin he
    killed!
And all the birds mourned that his blood was so
    spilled.

# RHYMES

MOTHER GOOSE

As Tommy Snooks, and Bessie Brooks
Were walking out one Sunday;
Says Tommy Snooks to Bessie Brooks,
" To-morrow will be Monday."

Jack Sprat could eat no fat,
His wife could eat no lean;
And so between them both,
They licked the platter clean.

Daffy-down-dilly has come up to town,
In a yellow petticoat and a green gown.

# SOLOMON GRUNDY

Mother Goose

Solomon Grundy,
Born on a Monday,
Christened on Tuesday,
Married on Wednesday,
Took ill on Thursday,
Worse on Friday,
Died on Saturday,
Buried on Sunday;
This is the end
Of Solomon Grundy.

# DARIUS GREEN AND HIS FLYING-MACHINE

### JOHN TOWNSEND TROWBRIDGE

IF ever there lived a Yankee lad,
Wise or otherwise, good or bad,
Who, seeing the birds fly, didn't jump
With flapping arms from stake or stump,
  Or, spreading the tail
  Of his coat for a sail,
Take a soaring leap from post or rail,
  And wonder why
  *He* couldn't fly,
And flap and flutter and wish and try,—
If ever you knew a country dunce
Who didn't try that as often as once,
All I can say is, that's a sign
He never would do for a hero of mine.

An aspiring genius was D. Green:
The son of a farmer,—age fourteen;
His body was long and lank and lean,—
Just right for flying, as will be seen;
He had two eyes, each bright as a bean,
And a freckled nose that grew between,

183

A little awry,—for I must mention
That he had riveted his attention
Upon his wonderful invention,
Twisting his tongue as he twisted the strings,
Working his face as he worked the wings,
And with every turn of gimlet and screw
Turning and screwing his mouth round too.
      Till his nose seemed bent
      To catch the scent,
Around some corner, of new-baked pies,
And his wrinkled cheeks and his squinting eyes
Grew puckered into a queer grimace,
That made him look very droll in the face,
      And also very wise.

And wise he must have been, to do more
Than ever a genius did before,
Excepting Dædalus of yore
And his son Icarus, who wore
      Upon their backs
      Those wings of wax
He had read of in the old almanacs.
Darius was clearly of the opinion,
That the air is also man's dominion,
And that, with paddle or fin or pinion,
      We soon or late
      Shall navigate

The azure as now we sail the sea.
The thing looks simple enough to me;
  And if you doubt it,
Hear how Darius reasoned about it.


  " Birds can fly,
   An' why can't I?
   Must we give in,"
   Says he with a grin,
  " 'T the bluebird an' phœbe
   Are smarter'n we be?
Jest fold our hands an' see the swaller
An' blackbird an' catbird beat us holler?
Does the leetle chatterin', sassy wren,
No bigger'n my thumb, know more than men?
   Jest show me that!
   Er prove 't the bat
Hez got more brains than's in my hat,
An' I'll back down, an' not till then! "


He argued further: " Ner I can't see
What's th' use o' wings to a bumble-bee,
Fer to git a livin' with, more'n to me;—
   Ain't my business
   Important's his'n is?

" That Icarus
   Was a silly cuss,—
Him an' his daddy Dædalus.
They might 'a' knowed wings made o' wax
Wouldn't stan' sun-heat an' hard whacks.
    I'll make mine o' luther,
    Er suthin' er other."


And he said to himself, as he tinkered and
    planned:
" But I ain't goin' to show my hand
To nummies that never can understand
The fust idee that's big an' grand.
    They'd 'a' laft an' made fun
O' Creation itself afore 'twas done! "
So he kept his secret from all the rest,
Safely buttoned within his vest;
And in the loft above the shed
Himself he locks, with thimble and thread
And wax and hammer and buckles and screws,
And all such things as geniuses use;—
Two bats for patterns, curious fellows!
A charcoal-pot and a pair of bellows;
An old hoop-skirt or two, as well as
Some wire, and several old umbrellas;
A carriage-cover, for tail and wings;

A piece of harness; and straps and strings;
>     And a big strong box,
>     In which he locks
These and a hundred other things.

His grinning brothers, Reuben and Burke
And Nathan and Jotham and Solomon, lurk
Around the corner to see him work,—
Sitting cross-legged, like a Turk,
Drawing the waxed end through with a jerk,
And boring the holes with a comical quirk
Of his wise old head, and a knowing smirk.
But vainly they mounted each other's backs,
And poked through knot-holes and pried
>     through cracks;
With wood from the pile and straw from
>     the stacks
He plugged the knot-holes and calked the
>     cracks;
And a bucket of water, which one would think
He had brought up into the loft to drink
>     When he chanced to be dry,
>     Stood always nigh,
>     For Darius was sly!
And whenever at work he happened to spy
At chink or crevice a blinking eye,
He let a dipper of water fly.

" Take that! an' ef ever ye git a peep,
  Guess ye'll ketch a weasel asleep!"
    And he sings as he locks
    His big strong box:

### Song

" The weasel's head is small an' trim,
An' he is leetle an' long an' slim,
An' quick of motion an' nimble of limb,
    An' ef yeou'll be
    Advised by me,
Keep wide awake when ye're ketchin' him!"

    So day after day
He stitched and tinkered and hammered away,
    Till at last 'twas done,—
The greatest invention under the sun!
" An' now," says Darius, " hooray fer some
    fun!"

    'Twas the Fourth of July,
    And the weather was dry,
And not a cloud was on all the sky,
Save a few light fleeces, which here and there,
    Half mist, half air,
Like foam on the ocean went floating by:
Just as lovely a morning as ever was seen
For a nice little trip in a flying-machine.

Thought cunning Darius: " Now I sha'n't go
Along 'ith the fellers to see the show.
I'll say I've got sich a terrible cough!
An' then, when the folks 'ave all gone off,
  I'll hev full swing
  Fer to try the thing,
An' practyse a leetle on the wing."

" Ain't goin' to see the celebration? "
Says Brother Nate. " No; botheration!
I've got sich a cold—a toothache—I—
My gracious!—feel's though I should fly! "

  Said Jotham, " 'Sho!
  Guess ye better go."
  But Darius said, " No!
Shouldn't wonder 'f yeou might see me,
  though,
'Long 'bout noon, ef I git red
O' this jumpin', thumpin' pain 'n my head."
For all the while to himself he said:

  " I tell ye what!
I'll fly a few times around the lot,
To see how 't seems, then soon's I've got
The hang o' the thing, ez likely's not,
  I'll astonish the nation,
  An' all creation,

By flyin' over the celebration!
Over their heads I'll sail like an eagle;
I'll balance myself on my wings like a sea-gull;
I'll dance on the chimbleys; I'll stan' on
    the steeple;
I'll flop up to winders an' scare the people!
I'll light on the libbe'ty-pole, an' crow;
An' I'll say to the gawpin' fools below:
    ' What world's this 'ere
      That I've come near? '
Fer I'll make 'em b'lieve I'm a chap f'm the
    moon!
An' I'll try a race 'ith their ol' bulloon."


    He crept from his bed;
And, seeing the others were gone, he said,
" I'm a-gittin' over the cold 'n my head."
    And away he sped,
To open the wonderful box in the shed.


His brothers had walked but a little way
When Jotham to Nathan chanced to say,
" What on airth is he up to, hey? "
" Don'o',—the' 's suthin' er other to pay,
  Er he wouldn't 'a' stayed to hum to-day."
Says Burke, " His toothache's all 'n his eye!

*He* never'd miss a Fo'th-o'-July
Ef he hedn't got some machine to try."
Then Sol, the little one, spoke: " By darn!
Le's hurry back an' hide 'n the barn,
An' pay him fer tellin' us that yarn!"
" Agreed!" Through the orchard they creep
      back,
Along by the fences, behind the stack,
And one by one, through a hole in the wall,
In under the dusty barn they crawl,
Dressed in their Sunday garments all;
And a very astonishing sight was that
When each in his cobwebbed coat and hat
Came up through the floor like an ancient rat.
       And there they hid;
       And Reuben slid
The fastenings back, and the door undid.
    " Keep dark!" said he,
" While I squint an' see what the' is to see."

As knights of old put on their mail,—
      From head to foot
      An iron suit,
Iron jacket and iron boot,
Iron breeches, and on the head
No hat, but an iron pot instead,
      And under the chin the bail,—

I believe they called the thing a helm;
And the lid they carried they called a shield;
And, thus accoutred, they took the field,
Sallying forth to overwhelm
The dragons and pagans that plague the
    realm:—
      So this modern knight
      Prepared for flight,
Put on his wings and strapped them tight;
Jointed and jaunty, strong and light;
Buckled them fast to shoulder and hip,—
Ten feet they measured from tip to tip!
And a helm had he, but that he wore
Not on his head like those of yore,
      But more like the helm of a ship.


      " Hush! " Reuben said,
      " He's up in the shed!
He's opened the winder,—I see his head!
      He stretches it out,
      An' pokes it about,
Lookin' to see 'f the coast is clear,
      An' nobody near;—
Guess he don'o' who's hid in here!
He's riggin' a spring-board over the sill!
Stop laffin, Solomon!  Burke, keep still!

He's a-climbin' out now—Of all the things!
What's he got on? I van, it's wings!
An' that 'tother thing? I vum, it's a tail!
An' there he sets like a hawk on a rail!
Steppin' careful, he travels the length
Of his spring-board, and teeters to try its
    strength.
Now he stretches his wings, like a monstrous
    bat;
Peeks over his shoulder, this way an' that,
Fer to see 'f the' 's any one passin' by;
But the' 's on'y a ca'f an' a goslin' nigh.
*They* turn up at him a wonderin' eye,
To see —— The dragon! he's goin' to fly!
Away he goes! Jimminy! what a jump!
    Flop—flop—an' plump
    To the ground with a thump!
Flutt'rin' an' flound'rin', all 'n a lump!"


As a demon is hurled by an angel's spear,
Heels over head, to his proper sphere,—
Heels over head, and head over heels,
Dizzily down the abyss he wheels,—
So fell Darius. Upon his crown,
In the midst of the barnyard, he came down,
In a wonderful whirl of tangled strings,

Broken braces and broken springs,
Broken tail and broken wings,
Shooting-stars, and various things!
Away with a bellow fled the calf,
And what was that? Did the gosling laugh?
  'Tis a merry roar
  From the old barn-door,
And he hears the voice of Jotham crying,
"Say, D'rius! how de yeou like flyin'?"

Slowly, ruefully, where he lay,
Darius just turned and looked that way,
As he stanched his sorrowful nose with his cuff.
"Wall, I like flyin' well enough,"
He said; "but the' ain't sich a thunderin' sight
O' fun in 't when ye come to light."

### MORAL

I just have room for the moral here:
And this is the moral,—Stick to your sphere.
Or if you insist, as you have the right,
On spreading your wings for a loftier flight,
The moral is,—Take care how you light.

# LITTLE ORPHANT ANNIE

## James Whitcomb Riley

Little Orphant Annie's come to our house to stay,
An' wash the cups an' saucers up, an' brush the
    crumbs away,
An' shoo the chickens off the porch, an' dust the
    hearth, an' sweep,
An' make the fire, an' bake the bread, an' earn her
    board-an'-keep;
An' all us other children, when the supper things
    is done,
We set around the kitchen fire an' has the mostest
    fun
A-list'nin' to the witch-tales 'at Annie tells about,
An' the gobble-uns 'at gits you
                        Ef you
                            Don't
                                Watch
                                    Out!

Onc't they was a little boy wouldn't say his
    pray'rs—·
An' when he went to bed at night, away up-stairs,

His mammy heered him holler, an' his daddy heered
    him bawl,
An' when they turn't the kivvers down he wasn't
    there at all!
An' they seeked him in the rafter-room, an' cubby-
    hole, an' press,
An' seeked him up the chimbly-flue, an' ever'-
    wheres, I guess;
But all they ever found was thist his pants an'
    roundabout!
An' the gobble-uns'll git you

               Ef you
                   Don't
                      Watch
                         Out!


An' one time a little girl 'ud allus laugh an' grin,
An' make fun of ever'one an' all her blood an' kin;
An' onc't when they was " company," an' ole folks
    was there,
She mocked 'em an' shocked 'em, an' said she didn't
    care!
An' thist as she kicked her heels, an' turn't to run
    an' hide,
They was two great big black things standin' by her
    side,

An' they snatched her through the ceilin' 'fore she
    knowed what she's about!
An' the gobble-uns'll git you
                Ef you
                    Don't
                        Watch
                            Out!

An' little Orphant Annie says, when the blaze is
    blue,
An' the lamp-wick sputters, an' the wind goes
    woo-oo!
An' you hear the crickets quit, an' the moon is gray,
An' the lightnin'-bugs in dew is all squenched
    away—
You better mind yer parents, an' yer teachers fond
    an' dear,
An' churish them 'at loves you, an' dry the or-
    phant's tear,
An' he'p the pore an' needy ones 'at clusters all
    about,
Er the gobble-uns'll git you
                Ef you
                    Don't
                      Watch
                          Out!

# THE SUICIDAL CAT

## Carolyn Wells

A LITTLE cat whose heart was broke
    Sat down one day and cried,
And with a deep, despairing sigh
    Resolved on suicide.
Saying, " Nobody in the world
    Would mourn me if I died!"


Nine lives the little cat had.
    Oh, his was a direful fate.
But he was cool and self-possessed,
    Extremely up-to-date;
He fired a well-aimed pistol-shot,
    And then his lives were eight.


His deadly purpose faltered not.
    That night about eleven
He shut his door, turned on the gas,
    And rolled his eyes toward heaven.
The night wore on.  When morning came
    His little lives were seven.

Next night the reckless little cat
   Again approached the Styx;
He tied around his slender neck
   Two awful heavy bricks.
A splash, a choke, a gurgle, and
   His lives were then but six.

"Confound it!" cried the little cat,
   "Why must I stay alive?
Is there no efficacious death,
   From which I can't revive?"
He bought a rope and hanged himself,
   But still his lives were five.

Then fiercely raged the little cat,
   And wickedly he swore,
He grasped the great big carving-knife
   And finished one life more;
And then he wondered how on earth
   He'd fix the other four.

A while he pondered thoughtfully,
   Then said, "It seems to me
To meet a passing railroad train
   Expedient would be."
Suiting the action to the word,
   The cat's lives now were three.

When he got up and shook himself,
   He felt a trifle blue.
" Mine is indeed a strenuous death,"
   He said.  " What can I do?
Aha! some nitro-glycerine! "
   Full soon his lives were two.

" Well," he remarked contentedly,
   " The deed is almost done;
I've very nearly severed
   The thread the Fates have spun."
A teaspoonful of poison next
   Reduced his lives to one.

A grin of satisfaction
   Across his features spread.
" Now for the grand finale! "
   The little cat then said.
He bought an automobile.   Soon
   The little cat was dead.

# THE WRECK OF THE *JULIE PLANTE*

William H. Drummond

On wan dark night on Lac St. Pierre,
    De win' she blow, blow, blow,
An' de crew of de wood scow *Julie Plante*
    Got scar't an' run below—
For de win' she blow lak hurricane;
    Bimeby she blow some more,
An' de scow bus' up on Lac St. Pierre
    Wan arpent from de shore.

De captinne walk on de fronte deck,
    An' walk de hin' deck too—
He call de crew from up de hole,
    He call de cook also.
De cook she's name was Rosie,
    She come from Montreal,
Was chambre maid on lumber barge,
    On de Grande Lachine Canal.

De win' she blow, from nor'—eas'—wes',—
    De sout' win' she blow, too,
W'en Rosie cry, " Mon Cher Captinne,
    Mon Cher, w'at I shall do? "

Den de captinne t'row de big ankerre,
  But still de scow she dreef,
De crew he can't pass on de shore,
  Becos he los' hees skeef.

De night was dark lak wan black cat,
  De wave run high an' fas',
W'en de captinne tak' de Rosie girl
  An' tie her to de mas'.
Den he also tak' de life-preserve,
  An' jomp off on de lak',
An' say, " Good-bye, ma Rosie dear,
  I go drown for your sak'."

Nex' morning very early
  'Bout ha'f-pas' two—t'ree—four—
De captinne—scow—an' de poor Rosie
  Was corpses on de shore.
For de win' she blow lak' hurricane,
  Bimeby she blow some more,
An' de scow, bus' up on Lac St. Pierre,
  Wan arpent from de shore.

### Moral

Now all good wood scow sailor man
  Tak' warning by dat storm
An' go an' marry some nice French girl
  An' live on wan beeg farm.

De win' can blow lak' hurricane
    An' s'pose she blow some more,
You can't get drown on Lac St. Pierre
    So long you stay on shore.

# THE YONGHY-BONGHY-BO

## Edward Lear

I really don't know any author to whom I am half so grateful for my idle self as Edward Lear.

JOHN RUSKIN.

On the Coast of Coromandel
    Where the early pumpkins blow,
In the middle of the woods
    Lived the Yonghy-Bonghy-Bo.
Two old chairs—and half a candle,
    One old jug without a handle,—
These were all his worldly goods:
    In the middle of the woods;
These were all the worldly goods
    Of the Yonghy-Bonghy-Bo,
Of the Yonghy-Bonghy-Bo.

Once, among the Bong-trees walking
    Where the early pumpkins blow,
To a little heap of stones
    Came the Yonghy-Bonghy-Bo.
There he heard a Lady talking,
    To some milk-white Hens of Dorking,—

" 'Tis the Lady Jingly Jones!
    On that little heap of stones
  Sits the Lady Jingly Jones! "
    Said the Yonghy-Bonghy-Bo,
  Said the Yonghy-Bonghy-Bo.


" Lady Jingly!  Lady Jingly!
    Sitting where the pumpkins blow,
  Will you come and be my wife? "
    Said the Yonghy-Bonghy-Bo,
" I am tired of living singly,—
    On this coast so wild and shingly,—
  I'm a-weary of my life;
    If you'll come and be my wife,
  Quite serene would be my life! "
    Said the Yonghy-Bonghy-Bo,
  Said the Yonghy-Bonghy-Bo.


" On this Coast of Coromandel
    Shrimps and watercresses grow,
  Prawns are plentiful and cheap, "
    Said the Yonghy-Bonghy-Bo.
" You shall have my chairs and candle,
    And my jug without a handle!
  Gaze upon the rolling deep
    (Fish is plentiful and cheap):

As the sea, my love is deep!"
　　Said the Yonghy-Bonghy-Bo,
Said the Yonghy-Bonghy-Bo.


Lady Jingly answered sadly,
　　And her tears began to flow,—
" Your proposal comes too late,
　　Mr. Yonghy-Bonghy-Bo!
I would be your wife most gladly!"
　　(Here she twirled her fingers madly.)
" But in England I've a mate!
　　Yes! you've asked me far too late,
For in England I've a mate,
　　Mr. Yonghy-Bonghy-Bo!
Mr. Yonghy-Bonghy-Bo!


" Mr. Jones (his name is Handel,—
　　Handel Jones, Esquire & Co.)
Dorking fowls delights to send,
　　Mr. Yonghy-Bonghy-Bo!
Keep, oh, keep your chairs and candle,
　　And your jug without a handle,—
I can merely be your friend!
　　Mr. Yonghy-Bonghy-Bo!
Mr. Yonghy-Bonghy-Bo!

" Though you've such a tiny body,
  And your head so large doth grow,—
Though your hat may blow away,
  Mr. Yonghy-Bonghy-Bo!
Though you're such a Hoddy Doddy,
  Yet I wish that I could modi-
fy the words I needs must say!
  Will you please to go away?
That is all I have to say,
  Mr. Yonghy-Bonghy-Bo!
Mr. Yonghy-Bonghy-Bo! "


Down the slippery slopes of Myrtle,
  Where the early pumpkins blow,
To the calm and silent sea,
  Fled the Yonghy-Bonghy-Bo.
There, beyond the Bay of Gurtle,
  Lay a large and lively Turtle.
" You're the Cove," he said, " for me:
  On your back beyond the sea,
Turtle, you shall carry me! "
  Said the Yonghy-Bonghy-Bo,
Said the Yonghy-Bonghy-Bo.


Through the silent roaring ocean
  Did the Turtle swiftly go;

Holding fast upon his shell
   Rode the Yonghy-Bonghy-Bo.
With a sad primeval motion
   Toward the sunset isles of Boshen
Still the Turtle bore him well,
   Holding fast upon his shell.
"Lady Jingly Jones, farewell!"
   Sang the Yonghy-Bonghy-Bo,
Sang the Yonghy-Bonghy-Bo.

From the Coast of Coromandel
   Did that Lady never go,
On that heap of stones she mourns
   For the Yonghy-Bonghy-Bo.
On that Coast of Coromandel,
   In his jug without a handle
Still she weeps, and daily moans;
   On the little heap of stones
To her Dorking Hens she moans,
   For the Yonghy-Bonghy-Bo,
For the Yonghy-Bonghy-Bo.

# CONDITION AND WAY OF LIFE OF DON QUIXOTE OF LA MANCHA

## Miguel de Cervantes

In a certain village of La Mancha, whose name I will not recall, there lived not long ago a gentleman—one of those who keep a lance in the rack, an ancient target, a lean hackney, and a greyhound for coursing. A mess of somewhat more beef than mutton, a salad on most nights, a hotch-potch on Saturdays, lentils on Fridays, with the addition of a pigeon on Sundays, consumed three parts of his substance. The rest of it was spent in a doublet of fine broadcloth, a pair of velvet breeches for holidays, with slippers of the same, and his homespun of the finest, with which he decked himself on week-days. He kept at home a housekeeper, who was past forty, and a niece who had not yet reached twenty, besides a lad for the field and market, who saddled the nag and handled the pruning-hook.

The age of our gentleman bordered upon fifty years. He was of a vigorous constitution, spare of flesh, dry of visage, a great early-riser, and a lover of the chase.

Be it known, then, that this gentleman above mentioned, during the interval that he was idle, which was the greater part of the year, gave himself up to the reading of books of chivalries, with so much fervor and relish, that he almost entirely neglected the exercise of the chase and even the management of his estate. And to such a pitch did his curiosity and infatuation reach, that he sold many acres of arable land in order to buy romances of chivalry to read; and so he brought home as many of them as he could procure. And of all none seemed to him so good as those composed by the famous Feliciano de Silva, for their brilliancy of style and those entangled sentences seemed to him to be very pearls; and especially when he came to read of the passages of love, and cartels of defiance, wherein he often found written things like these: " The reason of the unreason which is done to my reason in such wise my reason debilitates, that with reason I complain of your beauteousness." And also when he read: " The lofty heavens which of your divinity do divinely fortify you with the constellations, and make you deserver of the deserts which your mightiness deserves."

Over these reasons our poor gentleman lost his senses, and he used to keep awake at night in trying to comprehend them, and in plucking out their meaning, which not Aristotle himself could extract or understand, were he to come to life for that special purpose.

In fine, our gentleman was so absorbed in these studies, that he passed his nights reading from eve to dawn, and his days from dark to dusk; and so with little sleep and much study his brain dried up, to the end that he lost his wits. He filled himself with the imagination of all that he read in the books; with enchantments, with quarrels, battles, challenges, wounds, amorous plaints, love's torments, and follies impossible. And so assured was he of the truth of all that mass of fantastic inventions of which he read, that for him there was no other history so certain. In short, his wits utterly wrecked, he fell into the strangest delusion ever madman conceived in the world, and this was, that it was fitting and necessary for him, as he thought, both for the augmenting of his honor and the service of the State, to make himself a Knight Errant, and travel through the world with his armor and his horse seeking for adventures, and to exercise himself in all that he had read that the Knight Errant practised, redressing all kinds of wrong, and placing himself in perils and passes by the surmounting of which he might achieve an everlasting name and fame. Already the poor man imagined himself, by the valor of his arm, crowned with, at the least, the Empire of Trebizond. And so, with these imaginations so delightful, rapt in the strange zest with which they inspired him, he made haste to give effect to what he desired. The first thing he did was to furbish up some armor which had belonged to his great-grandfathers, which, eaten with rust and covered with mould, had lain for ages, where it had been put away and forgotten, in a corner. He scoured and dressed it as well as he was able, but he saw that it had one great defect, which was that there was no covered helmet, but only a simple morion or headpiece. This his ingenuity supplied, for, with pieces of pasteboard, he fashioned a sort of half-beaver, which, fitted to the morion, gave it the appearance of a complete helmet. The fact is that, to prove it to be strong and able to stand the chance of a sword-cut, he drew his sword and gave it a couple of strokes, demolishing with the very first in a moment what had cost him a week to make. The ease with which he had knocked it to pieces not seeming to him good, in order to secure himself against this danger he set to making it anew, fitting some bars of iron within in such a manner as to leave him satisfied with his defence; and without caring to make a fresh trial of it, he constituted and accepted it for a very perfect good helmet. He then went to inspect his nag, a beast which appeared to him to surpass Alexander's Bucephalus and the Cid's Bavieca. Four days were spent by our gentleman in meditating on what name to give him; for, as he said to himself, it was not right that the steed of Knight so famous, and in himself so good, should be without a recognized appellation; and therefore he endeavored to fit him with one which should signify what he had been prior to his belonging to a Knight Errant, and what he was then; since he thought it but right that, the master having changed his condition, the horse should also change his name, and get him one sublime and high-sounding, as befitted the new order and the new office which he professed. And so, after many names which he devised, effaced, and rejected, amended, remade and unmade in his mind and fancy, finally he decided to call him ROZINANTE —a name, in his opinion, lofty, sonorous, and common hackney, significative of what his animal had been when he was a common hackney, before he became what he now was, before, and in front of, all the hackneys in the world.

Having given to his horse a name so much to his liking, he then desired to give one to himself, and the thinking of this cost him eight other days. At last he decided to call himself DON QUIXOTE.

Then recollecting that the valorous Amadis was not contented with calling himself simply Amadis, but added the name of his kingdom and native country, to make it famous, taking the name of Amadis of Gaul, so he desired, like a good knight, to add to his own the name of his native land, and call himself DON QUIXOTE OF LA MANCHA, whereby, to his seeming, he made lively proclamation of his lineage and his country and honored it by taking his surname therefrom.

His armor then being cleaned, his morion manufactured into a helmet, a name given to his horse, and himself confirmed with a new one, it struck him that he lacked nothing else than to look for a lady of whom to be enamored; for the Knight Errant without amour was a tree without leaves and without fruit, and a body without soul. He would say to himself, " Were I, for my sins, or through good luck, to encounter hereabouts some giant, as usually happens to Knights Errant, and to overthrow him at the onset, or cleave him through the middle of his body, or, in fine, vanquish him and make him surrender, would it not be well to have some one to whom to send him as a present, that he might enter and bend the knee before my sweet mistress, and say with humble and subdued voice, ' I am the giant Caraculiambro, lord of the island of Malindramia, whom the never-to-be-praised-as-he-deserves Knight, Don Quixote of La Mancha, vanquished in single combat—he who hath commanded me to present myself before your grace that your highness may dispose of me at your pleasure.' "

Oh, how our good knight was pleased with himself when he had delivered this speech!—and the more when he found one to whom to give the name of his lady. It happened, as the belief is, that in a village near his own there was a well-looking peasant girl, with whom he had once fallen in love, though it is understood that she never knew it or had proof thereof. Her name was Aldonza Lorenzo, and upon her he judged it fit to bestow the title of mistress of his fancy; and seeking for her a name which should not much belie her own, and yet incline and approach to that of a princess or great lady, he decided to call her DULCINEA DEL TOBOSO, for she was a native of EL TOBOSO—a name, in his opinion, musical, romantic, and significant, as were all which he had given to himself and his belongings.

## THE TERRIBLE AND NEVER-BEFORE IMAGINED ADVENTURE OF THE WINDMILLS

" Fortune is guiding our affairs better than we could have desired, for look yonder, friend Sancho, where thirty or more huge giants are revealed, with whom I intend to do battle, and take all their lives. With their spoils we will begin to enrich ourselves, for this is fair war, and it is doing God great service to clear this evil spawn from off the face of the earth."

" What giants? " asked Sancho Panza.

" Those thou seest there," replied his master, " with the long arms, which some of them are wont to have of two leagues' length."

" Take care, sir," cried Sancho, " for those we see yonder are not giants, but windmills, and what in them look like arms are the sails which, being whirled about by the wind, make the millstone to go."

" It is manifest," answered Don Quixote, " that thou art not experienced in this matter of adventures. They are giants, and if thou art afraid get thee away home and dispose thyself to prayer while I go to engage with them in fierce and unequal combat."

So saying, he clapped spurs to Rozinante, his steed, without heeding the cries which Sancho Panza, his squire, uttered, warning him that those he was going to encounter were beyond all doubt windmills and not giants. But he went on so fully persuaded that they were giants that he neither listened to the cries of his squire Sancho, nor stopped to mark what they were, but shouted to them in a loud voice:

" Fly not, cowards, vile creatures, for it is a single cavalier who assails you! "

A slight breeze having sprung up at this moment, the great sail-arms began to move, on perceiving which Don Quixote cried:

" Although ye should wield more arms than had the giant Briareus, ye shall pay for it! "

Saying this, and commending himself with his whole soul to his lady Dulcinea, beseeching her to succor him in this peril, well covered with his buckler, with his lance in rest, he charged at Rozinante's best gallop, and attacked the first mill before him and thrusting his lance into the sail the wind turned it with so much violence that the lance was shivered to pieces, carrying with it the horse and his rider, who was sent rolling over the plain sorely damaged.

Sancho Panza hastened to his master's help as fast as his ass could go, and when he came up he found the Knight unable to stir, such a shock had Rozinante given him in the fall.

" God bless me," cried Sancho, " did I not tell your worship to look to what you were doing, for they were nought but windmills? And nobody could mistake them but one who had other such in his head."

" Peace, friend Sancho," said Don Quixote; " for the things of war are more than other subject to continual mutation. And, moreover, I believe, and that is the truth, that the same sage Friston, who robbed me of my room and my books, hath turned these giants to windmills, in order to deprive me of the glory of their overthrow, so great is the enmity he bears to me; but in the upshot his evil arts shall little avail against the goodness of my sword."

" God send it as He will," answered Sancho; and helping him to rise, the Knight remounted Rozinante, whose shoulders were half dislocated.

# LEEDLE YAWCOB STRAUSS

## Charles Follen Adams

I haf von funny leedle poy,
  Vot comes schust to mine knee;
Der queerest schap, der createst rogue,
  As efer you dit see.
He runs, and schumps, and schmases dings
  In all barts off der house:
But vot off dot? He vas mine son,
  Mine leedle Yawcob Strauss.

He get der measles und der mumbs,
  Und eferyding dot's oudt;
He sbills mine glass off lager bier,
  Poots schnuff indo mine kraut.
He fills mine pipe mit Linburg cheese—
  Dot vas der roughest chouse;
I'd dake dot vrom no oder poy
  But leedle Yawcob Strauss.

He dakes der milk-ban for a dhrum,
  Und cuts mine cane in dwo,
To make der schticks to beat it mit—
  Mine cracious, dot vas drue!

219

I dinks mine hed vas schplit abart,
  He kicks oup sooch a touse:
But nefer mind; der poys vas few
  Like dot young Yawcob Strauss.

He asks me questions sooch as dese:
  Who baints mine nose so red?
Who vas it cuts dot schmoodth blace oudt
  Vrom der hair ubon mine hed?
Und vere dere plaze goes vrom der lamp
  Vene'er der glim I douse.
How gan I all dose dings eggsblain
  To dot schmall Yawcob Strauss?

I somedomes dink I schall go vild
  Mit sooch a grazy poy
Und vish vonce more I gould haf rest,
  Und beaceful dimes enshoy;
But ven he vas aschleep in ped
  So quiet as a mouse,
I prays der Lord, " Dake anyding,
  But leaf dot Yawcob Strauss."

# THE ENCHANTED SHIRT

### John Hay

The King was sick. His cheek was red,
  And his eye was clear and bright;
He ate and drank with a kingly zest,
  And peacefully snored at night.


But he said he was sick, and a king should know,
  And doctors came by the score.
They did not cure him. He cut off their heads,
  And sent to the schools for more.


At last two famous doctors came,
  And one was as poor as a rat,—
He had passed his life in studious toil,
  And never found time to grow fat.


The other had never looked in a book;
  His patients gave him no trouble;
If they recovered, they paid him well;
  If they died, their heirs paid double.

Together they looked at the royal tongue,
    As the King on his couch reclined;
In succession they thumped his august chest,
    But no trace of disease could find.


The old sage said, " You're as sound as a nut."
" Hang him up," roared the King in a gale—
In a ten-knot gale of royal rage;
    The other leech grew a shade pale;


But he pensively rubbed his sagacious nose,
    And thus his prescription ran—
*The King will be well, if he sleeps one night
    In the Shirt of a Happy Man.*


\*     \*     \*     \*     \*     \*     \*


Wide o'er the realm the couriers rode,
    And fast their horses ran,
And many they saw, and to many they spoke,
    But they found no Happy Man.


They saw two men by the roadside sit,
    And both bemoaned their lot;
For one had buried his wife, he said,
    And the other one had not.

At last they came to a village gate,
 A beggar lay whistling there;
He whistled, and sang, and laughed, and rolled
 In the grass in the soft June air.

The weary couriers paused and looked
 At the scamp so blithe and gay;
And one of them said, " Heaven save you, friend!
 You seem to be happy to-day."

" O yes, fair sirs," the rascal laughed,
 And his voice rang free and glad;
" An idle man has so much to do
 That he never has time to be sad."

" That is our man," the courier said;
 " Our luck has led us aright.
 I will give you a hundred ducats, friend,
 For the loan of your shirt to-night."

The merry blackguard lay back on the grass,
 And laughed till his face was black;
" I would do it, God wot," and he roared with the
   fun,
 " But I haven't a shirt to my back."

  *  *  *  *  *  *  *

Each day to the King the reports came in
  Of his unsuccessful spies,
And the sad panorama of human woes
  Passed daily under his eyes.

And he grew ashamed of his useless life,
  And his maladies hatched in gloom;
He opened his windows and let the air
  Of the free heaven into his room.

And out he went into the world, and toiled
  In his own appointed way;
And the people blessed him, the land was glad,
  And the King was well and gay.

# A STUDY IN PIRACY

### Josephine Dodge Daskam

It might not have occurred to you to find the Head Captain terrible to look upon, had you seen him first without his uniform. There seems to be something essentially pacific in the effect of a broad turn-over gingham collar, a blue neck-ribbon, and a wide straw hat: and you might be pardoned for thinking him a rather mild person. But could you have encountered him in a black cambric mask with pinked edges, a broad sash of Turkey red wound tightly about his waist, and that wide collar turned up above his ears—the tie conspicuous for its absence—you might have sung another tune. His appearance was at such a time nothing short of menacing.

The Lieutenant was distinctly less impressive. His sash, though not so long as the Head Captain's, was forever coming untied and trailing behind him, and as he often retreated rapidly, he stumbled and fell over it twice out of three times. This gave it a draggled and spiritless look. Moreover, he was not allowed to turn his collar up except on Saturdays, and the one his sister had made him from wrapping paper had an exotic, not to say amateur theatrical effect that was far from convincing. The eye-holes in his mask, too, were much too large —showing, indeed, the greater part of both cheeks, each of which was provided with a deep dimple. Seen in the daytime, he was not—to speak confidentially—very awesome.

As for the Vicar—well, there were obstacles in the way of her presenting such an appearance as she would have liked. In the first place, there was not enough Turkey red to go evenly around, and to her disgust she had been obliged to put up with a scant three-quarters of a yard—not a wide strip at that. What was by courtesy called the Vicar's waist was not far from three-quarters of a yard in circumference, which fact compelled her to strain her sash tightly in order to be able to make even a small hard knot, to say nothing of bows and ends. She had no collar of any kind—her frocks were gathered into bands at the neck—and she was not allowed to imitate the Lieutenant's: who, though generally speaking a mush of concession, held out very strongly for this outward and visible sign of a presumable inward and spiritual superiority. So the Vicar, in a wild attempt at masculinity, had privately borrowed a high linen collar of her uncle.

The shirts in her uncle's drawer had printed inside them, " *wear a seventeen-and-a-half collar with this shirt,*" so you will not be surprised to learn that the Vicar occasionally fell into the collar, so to speak, and found herself most effectually muzzled.

But the worst was her mask. Her hair came down in a heavy bang almost to her straight brown eyebrows: her round, brown eyes were somewhat short-sighted: her eye-holes were too small. In consequence of these facts, whenever it was desirable or necessary to see an inch before her nose she was obliged to push the mask up over her bang, when it waved straight out and up, and looked like some high priest's mitre.

Her title was due to her uncle, who to do him justice, was as innocent of his influence in the matter as of the loss of his collar.

" When a person isn't the head of the Pirates, but is an officer just the same, and has some say about things, what do you call that? " she asked him abruptly one day. He was reading at the time, and not unnaturally understood her to say " the head of a parish."

" Why, that's called a vicar, I suppose you mean," he answered.

" A vicker! Does he have some say? "

" Some *say?* "

" Yes "—impatiently—" some say. He hasn't got to do the way the others tell him *all* the time, has he? "

" Oh, dear, no. Don't you know Mr. Wright, down at the chapel? He's called the vicar. He really manages it, I think. Of course it's not like being the rector —— "

" Chapel? Is that the only kind of vicker, like Mr. Wight? "

" Why, of course not, silly! There are lots of different kinds."

" Oh," and she retired, practising the word. The others were much impressed by her cleverness in discovering such a fascinating title. It savored of *wicked* and *villain,* to begin with: and pursuing the advantage of their previous ignorance of it, she invented several privileges and perquisites of the office, which to deny would argue their lack of information on the subject, a thing she knew they would never own.

One of these was the right to summon the band, when the Head Captain had decided on an expedition, to any meeting-place she saw fit: and though in a great many ways her superiors found her a nuisance, the Lieutenant in particular objecting in a nagging, useless sort of way to most of her suggestions, they could not but admit that her selection of mysterious, unsuspected *rendezvous* was often brilliantly original.

On one especial occasion, a warm afternoon late in June, when the houses and yards were all quiet, and the very dogs lay still in the shade, the Vicar led them softly to the chicken yard, mystified them by crawling through a broken glass frame into the covered roost, crouching along beneath the perches, and going out again by the legitimate door without stopping to speak. This effectually silenced the Lieutenant—the chicken house seemed an old ruse to him, and he was sniffing in preparation for the expression of his opinion. Out across the yard and twice around an enormous hogshead they walked solemnly. Such a prelude must mean a great *finale,* and the Head Captain felt decidedly curious. The Vicar paused, made a short detour for the purpose of getting two empty boxes, piled them one on the other, and lightly swung herself into the cask. A loud thud announced her safe arrival at the bottom, and flushed with delight at the incomparable secrecy of the thing, the Head Captain followed her. The Lieutenant, grumbling as usual, and very nearly hanging himself in his sash, which caught on the edge, tumbled after, and standing close together in the great barrel they grinned consciously at each other.

The Head Captain broke the silence.

" Are we all here? " he demanded, his voice waking strange and hollow echoes.

" Yes! " replied the Vicar delightedly, bursting with pride.

" Aye, aye! " said the Lieutenant with careful formality.

" Then listen here! " the Head Captain spoke in a hoarse whisper. " This'll be a diff'rent way. This is going to be the real thing. To-day *we're going to steal!* "

The Vicar gasped. " Really steal? " she whispered.

" Steal what? " said the Lieutenant with a noncommittal gruffness.

" I don't know till I get there," replied the Head Captain grandly. " Gold, I suppose, or treasures or something like that. Of course, if we're caught ——"

The Lieutenant sucked in his breath with a peculiar whistling noise—one of his most envied accomplishments—and ran his finger-nail with a grating sound around his side of the barrel.

" Jim Elder stole some apples from my father's barn, and my father licked him good," he suggested.

" Apples! Apples! " The Head Captain frowned

terribly, adding with biting irony: " I s'pose Jim Elder's a Pirate!  I s'pose he wears a uniform!  I s'pose he knows the ways this gang knows!  I s'pose he meets in a barrel like this!  Huh?"

There was no answer, and the Head Captain settled his mask more firmly.  " Come on!" he said.

They looked at the sharp edge of the hogshead; it was far away.  They looked inquiringly at the Vicar; she dropped her eyes.  Oh, Woman, in your hours of ease you can devise fine secret places, you can lead us to them, but can you bring us back to the outer world and the reality you seduced us from?  There was an embarrassing pause.  The seconds seemed hours.  Would they die in this old, smelly barrel?

The Head Captain smiled to himself.

" I guess you kids never'd git out o' here unless I showed you how!" he remarked cheerfully.

" Forward!  March!" He took the one step possible, and scowled because they did not follow him.

" Don't you see?" he said irritably.  " When I say ' three,' fall over.  Now, one—two—*three!*"

He pushed the Lieutenant and the Vicar against the side of the barrel, and precipitated himself against them.  The barrel wavered, tottered, and fell with a bang on its side, the subordinate officers jouncing and gasping, unhappy cushions for their Head Captain, who crawled out over them, adjusted his collar, and strode off across the chicken yard.  At the gate they caught up with him.

" Lieutenant! "

" Aye, aye, sir."

" Go straight ahead and watch out for us. Whistle three times if the coast is clear.  Beware of—of anything you see."

" Aye, aye, sir."

The Lieutenant slunk off, a peculiar caution in the slope of his shoulders and his long, noiseless stride.  He rounded the barn and disappeared from sight.  There was a moment of suspense. Suddenly he appeared again, his hand raised warningly.

" Sst, sst! " he hissed.

Promptly they skipped behind the wood-house door.  In a moment a man's footsteps were audible; somebody was swinging by the barn, whistling as he went.  He called out to the cook as he went by: " Pretty hot, ain't it?  Hey!  I say it's pretty hot! "

He was gone.  He had absolutely no idea of their presence.  The first of the delicious thrills had begun.  The Lieutenant, from his post behind

the barn door, could have leaned out and touched
him, but he had no idea. From that moment the
scenery changed. The yard was enchanted ground,
the buildings strange and doubtful, the stretches
between haven and haven full of dangers.

Presently three soft whistles broke the silence.
They glided out around the barn, and scaled the
first fence. The Head Captain stopped to caution,
the Lieutenant became hopelessly complicated in
his sash, so the Vicar got over first. Though
plump, she was light on her feet, and had been
known to push the others over in her nervous haste;
she threw herself upon a solid board fence in an
utterly reckless way, striking the top flat on her
stomach, and sliding, slipping down the other side.
Her method, thoroughly ridiculous and unscien-
tific as it was, invariably succeeded, and she usually
waited a few seconds for them after picking herself
up. When one climbs after the most approved
fashion, employing as few separate motions as possible, making every one tell, the result of such
slippery, panting scrambles as the Vicar's is particularly irritating. The success of the amateur is
never pardonable.

" Which way, Head Captain? "

A dusty forefinger indicated the neighboring
barn.

" Secret way or door? "

" Secret way."

They cast hurried glances about them: nobody was in sight.   At the corner of the barn the Lieutenant again performed scout duty, and his three whistles brought them to a back entrance hardly noticeable to the chance explorer of stable yards— a low door into a disused cow-house.

Softly they stole in, softly peeped into the barn. It lay placid and empty, smelling of leather and hay and horses, with barrels of grain all about, odd bits of harness, and tins of wagon grease, wisps of straw, and broken tools scattered over the floor. Broad bands of sunlight streaked everything. They crept through a lane of barrels, and mounted a rickety stair, heart in mouth.   Who might be at the top?

A moment's pause, and then the Head Captain nodded.

" All right, men," he breathed.

Then went carefully through the thick hay that strewed the upper floor, avoiding the cracks and pits that loosened boards and decayed planking offered the unwary foot.   With unconscious directness the Lieutenant turned to the great pile of hay that usually marked the end of this expedition, but the Head Captain frowned and passed by the short

ladder that led to the summit.   He pushed through
an avenue of old machinery, crawled over two old
sleighs and under a grind-stone frame, and emerged
into a dim, almost empty corner.

The heat of the hay was intense.   The stuffy,
dry smell of it filled their nostrils.   Where the
bright, wide ray of sunlight fell from the little window in the apex, the air was seen to be dancing and
palpitating with millions of tiny particles that kept
up a continuous churning motion.   The perspira-
tion dripped from the Vicar's round cheeks: she
panted with the heat.

Walking on his tiptoes, the Head Captain
sought the darkest depths of the corner, stumbling
over an old covered chest.   He stopped, he put his
hand on the lid.   The two attendant officers gasped.
The Head Captain, with infinite caution, lifted that
lid.

Suddenly a dull, echoing crash shook the floor.
The Vicar squeaked in nervous terror.   I say
squeaked, because with grand presence of mind the
Lieutenant smothered her certain scream in the
folds of his ever-ready sash, and only a faint chirp
disturbed the deathly silence that followed the
crash.   The Head Captain's hand trembled, but he
held the cover of the chest and waited.   Again
that hollow boom, followed by a rustling, as of hay

being dragged down, and a champing, swallowing, gurgling sound.

"Nothin' but the horses," whispered the Lieutenant, removing his sash. "Shut up, now!"

The Vicar breathed again. The Head Captain bent over the chest.

"Oh! Oh! Oh! Oh, fellows! Look-a-here!" His voice shook. His eyes stared wide. They crept nearer and caught big breaths.

There in the old chest, carelessly thrown together, uncovered, unprotected, lay a glittering wealth of strange gold and silver treasures. Knobs, cups, odd pieces, shallow saucers, countless rings as big as small cookies, plain bars of metal, heavy rods.

The Head Captain's eyes shone feverishly, he breathed quick.

"Here, here, here!" he whispered, and thrust his hands into the box. He ladled out a handful to the Vicar. For a moment she shrank away; and then, as a shallow, carved gold-colored thing touched her hand, her cheeks heated red, she seized it, and hid it in her pocket.

"Gimme another," she begged softly, "gimme that shiny, little cup!"

If there had been any doubt as to the heavenly reality of the thing, it was all over now. No more

need the Head Captain's swelling words fill out
the bare gaps of the actual state of the case.    Here
were the things—this was no pretend-game.    Here
was danger, here was crime, here was glittering
wealth all unguarded, and no one knew but them!

They gloated over the chest: their hot fingers
handled eagerly every ring and big chain.    Only
the Lieutenant, sucking in his breath, excitedly
broke the ecstatic silence.

The Head Captain first mastered himself.

" Hm, that's enough—*from here!* " he commanded with dreadful implication.    " Come on.
They'll kill us if they catch us!    Soft, now.    Don't
breathe so loud, Vicar! "

Off in a different direction he led them, having
closed the box softly, and instead of making for the
stairs, stopped before three square openings in the
floor.    He lay flat on his stomach and peered down
one.    It opened directly above the manger, and
when he had cast down two armfuls of hay and
measured the distance with his eye, they saw he
meant to drop through, and realized that his blood
was up, and heaven knew where he would stop that
day.

The Vicar caught the idea before the Lieutenant,
and with characteristic impatience, was through the
second hole before the third member of the band had

thrown down his first armful.  Light as a cat she dropped, scrambled out of the manger, and as a step sounded in the outer barn, dragged the Lieutenant through in an agony of apprehension, stumbled across the great heap of stable refuse, and crouched, palpitating, behind the cow-house door.

The Head Captain, whom crises calmed and immediate danger heartened, himself crept back into the stable to gather from the sound of the steps the direction taken by the intruder.

He was talking to the horse.

"Want some dinner?  I'll bet you do.  Stealing hay, was you?  That'll never do."

It was enough.  Soon he would go up-stairs to count over the treasures—who would ever have supposed that this simple-looking stableman had known for years of such a trove?—and then woe to the Pirates!

"Come on, you!  Run for your life!" he shot at them, and they tore across the yard, over a back fence, and across a vacant lot, panting, stumbling, muttering to each other, the Vicar crying with excitement.  The Lieutenant caught his foot in his sash and fell miserably, mistaking them for arms of the law, as they loyally turned back to pick him up, and fighting them with feeble punches.  They dragged him through a hedge and took refuge in an old tool-house.

Slowly they got back breath. The delicious horror of pursuit was lifted from them. It appeared that they were safe.

" You goin' home, now? " said the Lieutenant huskily.

Home? Home? Was the fellow mad? The Head Captain vouchsafed no answer.

" Forward! March! "

He strode out of the tool-house and made for the barn. A large dog barked, and a voice called:

" Down, Danny, Down! "

They returned hastily, and climbed laboriously out of a little window on the other side of the tool-house, striking a bee-line for the adjoining property. The new treasure jingled in their pockets as they ran stealthily into this barn. The last restraint was cast away, they were on new territory. A succession of back-yard cuts had resulted in their turning a corner, and had they gone openly and in the light of the day out into the street, they would have found themselves in another part of the town. The Captain crept in a low window. He was entirely wrapped up in his dreadful character. Blind to consequences, hardly looking to see if the others followed him, he worked his way over the sill and stared about him. Imagination was no longer necessary. No fine-spun trickery was needed to turn the too-familiar places into weird dens, the well-known barns into menacing danger-traps. Here all was new, untried, of endless possibilities.

It was a clean, spacious spot. Great shadowy, white-draped carriages stood along the sides: a smell of varnish and new leather prevailed. On the walls hung fascinating garden tools: quaint-nosed watering-pots, coils of hose, a lawn fountain. All was still. The Head Captain strode across the floor, extending his hand with a majestic sweep.

"All these things—all of 'em—anything we want, we can take!" he muttered, but not to them. They could plainly see he was talking to himself. Rapt in wild dreams of unchecked depredation he stamped about, fingering the garden hose, prying behind the carriages, tossing his head and breathing hard.

Suddenly came a step as of a man walking on gravel. It drew nearer, nearer. For one awful moment the Lieutenant seemed in danger of thinking himself a frightened little boy in a strange barn: he plucked at his sash nervously. The next instant two hands fell from opposite directions on his shoulders.

"Get into a carriage—quick, quick, quick!"

hissed the Head Captain, and he heard the Vicar
panting as she shoved him under the flap of the
sheet that draped a high-swung victoria. She was
with him, huddled close beside him on the floor of
the carriage, and it seemed hardly credible that
the clatter of the Head Captain's hasty dive into
the neighboring surrey could have failed to catch
the ear of the man who entered the barn. But he
heard nothing. He walked by them lazily, he
paused and struck a match on the wheel of the
victoria, and the smell of tobacco crept in under the
sheet. It seemed to the Vicar that the thumping of
her heart must shake the carriage. She dared not
gasp for breath, but she knew she should burst if
that man stood there much longer. It could not be
possible that he wouldn't find them. Ah, how little
he knew! Right under his very pipe lay those who
could take away everything in his old barn if they
chose. Perhaps the very surrey that now held that
terrible Head Captain might be gone ere morning,
he had such ambitions, such vaulting dreams.

Thump! Thump! Thump! went her heart,
and the Lieutenant's breath whistled through his
teeth. Never in their lives had such straining excitement possessed their every nerve. Oh, go on,
go on, or we shall scream!

He sauntered by, he opened some door at the

rear. The latch all but clicked, when a hollow but unmistakable sneeze burst from the Head Captain's surrey. Immediately the door opened again. The man took a step back. All was deathly still; the echoes of their leader's fateful sneeze thrilled the hearts of his anguished followers.

"Humph!" muttered a deep voice, "that's queer. Anybody out there?"

Silence. Silence that buzzed and hummed and roared in the Vicar's ears.

"Queer—I thought I heard . . . Queer!" muttered the man. The Lieutenant shuddered.

Again the latch clicked. After an artful pause the nose of the Head Captain appeared, inserted at an angle between the two sheets that draped the surrey. Cautiously he swung himself down, cautiously he tiptoed toward the others.

"Ssh! Ssh! All safe!" he whispered. They scrambled out, and a glance at his reserved frown taught them that the recent sneeze must not be mentioned.

Like cats they crept up the stairs, and only the Head Captain's great presence of mind prevented their falling backward down the flight, for there on the hay before them lay a man stretched at full length, breathing heavily. His face was a deep red in color, and a strong, sweetish odor filled the loft. They turned about at the Head Captain's warning gesture, and waited while he stole fearfully up and examined the man. When he rejoined them there was a new triumph in his eyes, a greater exaltation in his hurried speech.

" Come here, Lieutenant! "

" Aye, aye, sir."

" This is a dead pirate. He died defending—defending his life. He will be discovered if we leave him here."

This seemed eminently probable. The Lieutenant looked alarmed. He took a step or two on the loft floor and returned relieved.

" No, he ain't dead either," he announced, " he's only as —— "

" He is dead," repeated the Head Captain firmly. " Dead, I say. You shut up, will you? And we must bury him."

The Lieutenant looked sulky and chewed the end of his sash. To be so put down before the Vicar! It was hardly decent. And she, in her usual and irritating way, grasped the situation immediately.

" We must bury him right off," she whispered excitedly, " before that man gets up here."

" That man," added the Head Captain, " is a dreadful bad fellow, I tell you. If he was to catch us up here, I don't know—I don't know but he'd—here, come back, Lieutenant! Come back, I say!"

They stole up to the dead pirate, who had not the appearance attributed by popular imagination to those who have died nobly. The Lieutenant was frankly in the dark as to his superior officer's intentions.

"If you take him off and bury him he'll wake——"

"Hush your noise!" interrupted the Head Captain angrily.

The Vicar could not wait for any one else's initiative, but began feverishly pulling up handfuls of hay and piling them lightly over the dead pirate's boots. The Head Captain covered the man's body with two hastily snatched armfuls, and as the Vicar's courage gave out at this point, coolly laid a thin wisp directly over the red face. The pirate was buried. It gave one a thrill to see hardly a dim outline of his figure.

"Hats off, my men," whispered the Head Captain, hoarse with emotion.

"The last time I saw that pirate," he began.

The Lieutenant tripped, and sat down abruptly.

"The—the last time you saw him?" he stammered.

" That's what I said," responded the Head Captain shortly. " The last time I saw him I didn't s'pose I'd have to bury him. He'd just got a lot of treasures and stuff and —— Sst! Sst! For your lives! "

They scuttled off desperately. The ground was new to them, and had it not been for providential garbage barrels and outhouses, they could hardly have hoped to conceal themselves from the man who was raking up the yard. To avoid him they dashed straight through his barn, and rounded a summer-house without perceiving a small tea-party going on there, till they ran through it, to their own sick terror, and the abject amazement of the tea-party. They tore through a hedge, panted a doubtful moment in a woodhouse, then took up their headlong flight with the vague, straining pace of crowded dreams. On, on, on. Slip behind that lilac clump—wait. Sst! Sst! Then get along! Oh, hurry, hurry! Pick up your sash! Whose *is* this yard? Never mind! hurry!

They dropped exhausted under their own pear-tree.

" My, but that was a close shave! I thought they'd got us sure! " breathed the Head Captain.

" Wh-who were they? " asked the Lieutenant, round-eyed.

" Who were they?   Who were they? " the Head Captain repeated scornfully.  " The idea!  I guess you'd find out who they were if they caught you once! "

The Lieutenant shot a sly glance at the Vicar. Did she know?  You never could tell, she pretended so.  She shivered at the Head Captain's implication.

" Yes, sirree, I guess you'd find out then," she assured him.

Suddenly the Head Captain's face fell.  " The treasure! " he gasped.  " It's gone! "

In dismay they turned out their pockets.  All those vessels of gold and silver were lost—lost in that last mad rush.  All but the shallow, gold-colored saucer in the Vicar's hand.  They looked at it enviously, but honor kept them silent.  To the Vicar belonged the spoils.

" I don't see what good they were, anyhow," began the Lieutenant morosely.

" ' Good '? " mimicked the Head Captain, enraged.  " ' Good '?  Why, didn't we *steal* 'em? "

Slowly they took off their uniforms and hid them under the piazza.  Slowly the occasion faded into the light of common day: objects lost their mystery, the barn and the tool-house imperceptibly divested

themselves of all glamor.  It was only the back
yard.

The Head Captain and the Lieutenant threw
themselves down under the pear-tree again and fell
into a doze.  The Vicar, grasping her treasure,
stumbled up the back stairs and took an informal
nap on the landing.  It must have been at this time
that the gold-colored saucer slipped from her hand,
for when she woke on the sofa in the upper hall, it
was nowhere about.

The same hands that had transferred her to that
more conventional resting-place, bathed and attired
her for supper, and though two hours ago she would,
as a pirate, have exulted in her guilty possession,
somehow as a neat, small person in pink ribbons she
felt shy at approaching the subject, and ate her
custard in silence.

Some time during the hour of the next long
morning, as she played quietly on the piazza, she
caught her mother's voice, slightly raised to reach
the cook's ear:

"Why, I suppose it is, I shouldn't wonder,
Maggie.  I suppose the child picked it up somewhere.  Did you hear that, Fred, about Mr. Van
Tuyl's best harness?  All scattered through half
the back yards on Winter Street.  All those brass
ornaments and parts of the very side-lamps, too.

Take that piece, Maggie, and give it to the man when you see him."

The Vicar sighed. Just then she felt, with the poet, that home-keeping hearts are happiest.

# A TRAGIC STORY

### William Makepeace Thackeray

There lived a sage in days of yore,
And he a handsome pigtail wore;
But wondered much, and sorrowed more,
    Because it hung behind him.

He mused upon this curious case,
And swore he'd change the pigtail's place,
And have it hanging at his face,
    Not dangling there behind him.

Says he, " The mystery I've found;
I'll turn me round."   He turned him round,
    But still it hung behind him.

Then round and round, and out and in,
All day the puzzled sage did spin;
In vain—it mattered not a pin—
    The pigtail hung behind him.

And right and left, and round about,
And up and down, and in and out,
He turned; but still the pigtail stout
    Hung steadily behind him.

And though his efforts never slack,
And though he twist, and twirl, and tack,
Alas! still faithful to his back,
　　The pigtail hangs behind him.

# THE DIVERTING HISTORY OF
## JOHN GILPIN

### WILLIAM COWPER

JOHN GILPIN was a citizen
  Of credit and renown,
A train-band Captain eke was he
  Of famous London town.

John Gilpin's spouse said to her dear,
  Though wedded we have been
These twice ten tedious years, yet we
  No holiday have seen.

To-morrow is our wedding-day,
  And we will then repair
Unto the Bell at Edmonton,
  All in a chaise and pair.

My sister and my sister's child,
  Myself and children three,
Will fill the chaise, so you must ride
  On horseback after we.

He soon replied—I do admire
  Of womankind but one,
And you are she, my dearest dear,
  Therefore it shall be done.

I am a linen-draper bold,
  As all the world doth know.
And my good friend the Callender
  Will lend his horse to go.

Quoth Mrs. Gilpin—That's well said;
  And for that wine is dear,
We will be furnish'd with our own,
  Which is both bright and clear.

John Gilpin kiss'd his loving wife,
  O'erjoyed was he to find
That though on pleasure she was bent,
  She had a frugal mind.

The morning came, the chaise was brought,
  But yet was not allow'd
To drive up to the door, lest all
  Should say that she was proud.

So three doors off the chaise was stay'd,
  Where they did all get in,
Six precious souls, and all agog
  To dash through thick and thin.

Smack went the whip, round went the wheel,
    Were never folk so glad,
The stones did rattle underneath
    As if cheapside were mad.

John Gilpin at his horse's side
    Seized fast the flowing mane,
And up he got in haste to ride,
    But soon came down again.

For saddle-tree scarce reach'd had he,
    His journey to begin,
When turning round his head he saw
    Three customers come in.

So down he came, for loss of time,
    Although it grieved him sore,
Yet loss of pence, full well he knew,
    Would trouble him much more.

'Twas long before the customers
    Were suited to their mind,
When Betty screaming came down-stairs,
    " The wine is left behind."

Good lack! quoth he, yet bring it me,
    My leathern belt likewise,
In which I bear my trusty sword
    When I do exercise.

Now Mistress Gilpin, careful soul,
　　Had two stone bottles found,
To hold the liquor that she loved,
　　And keep it safe and sound.

Each bottle had a curling ear,
　　Through which the belt he drew,
And hung a bottle on each side
　　To make his balance true.

Then over all, that he might be
　　Equipped from top to toe,
His long red cloak well brush'd and neat
　　He manfully did throw.

Now see him mounted once again
　　Upon his nimble steed,
Full slowly pacing o'er the stones
　　With caution and good heed.

But finding soon a smoother road
　　Beneath his well-shod feet,
The snorting beast began to trot,
　　Which galled him in his seat.

So, fair and softly, John he cried,
　　But John he cried in vain,
That trot became a gallop soon
　　In spite of curb and rein.

So stooping down, as needs he must
   Who cannot sit upright,
He grasped the mane with both his hands
   And eke with all his might.

His horse, who never in that sort
   Had handled been before,
What thing upon his back had got
   Did wonder more and more.

Away went Gilpin, neck or nought,
   Away went hat and wig,
He little dreamt when he set out
   Of running such a rig.

The wind did blow, the cloak did fly,
   Like streamer long and gay,
Till loop and button failing both,
   At last it flew away.

Then might all people well discern
   The bottles he had slung,
A bottle swinging at each side
   As hath been said or sung.

The dogs did bark, the children scream'd,
   Up flew the windows all,
And every soul cried out, " Well done! "
   As loud as he could bawl.

Away went Gilpin—who but he;
   His fame soon spread around—
He carries weight, he rides a race,
   'Tis for a thousand pound.

And still as fast as he drew near,
   'Twas wonderful to view
How in a trice the turnpike-men
   Their gates wide open threw.

And now as he went bowing down
   His reeking head full low,
The bottles twain behind his back
   Were shatter'd at a blow.

Down ran the wine into the road,
   Most piteous to be seen,
Which made his horse's flanks to smoke
   As they had basted been.

But still he seem'd to carry weight,
   With leathern girdle braced,
For all might see the bottle-necks
   Still dangling at his waist.

Thus all through merry Islington
   These gambols he did play,
And till he came into the Wash
   Of Edmonton so gay.

And there he threw the Wash about
   On both sides of the way,
Just like unto a trundling mop,
   Or a wilde-goose at play.

At Edmonton his loving wife
   From the balcony spied
Her tender husband, wondering much
   To see how he did ride.

Stop, stop, John Gilpin!—Here's the
      house—
   They all at once did cry,
The dinner waits, and we are tired:
   Said Gilpin—so am I.

But yet his horse was not a whit
   Inclined to tarry there,
For why?  His owner had a house
   Full ten miles off, at Ware.

So like an arrow swift he flew
   Shot by an archer strong,
So did he fly—which brings me to
   The middle of my song.

Away went Gilpin, out of breath,
   And sore against his will,
Till at his friend's the Callender's
   His horse at last stood still.

The Callender, amazed to see
   His neighbor in such trim,
Laid down his pipe, flew to the gate,
   And thus accosted him—

What news? what news? your tidings tell,
   Tell me you must and shall—
Say why bare-headed you are come,
   Or why you come at all?

Now Gilpin had a pleasant wit
   And loved a timely joke,
And thus unto the Callender
   In merry guise he spoke—

I came because your horse would come;
   And if I well forebode,
My hat and wig will soon be here,
   They are upon the road.

The Callender, right glad to find
   His friend in merry pin,
Return'd him not a single word,
   But to the house went in.

Whence straight he came with hat and wig,
   A wig that flowed behind,
A hat not much the worse for wear,
   Each comely in its kind.

He held them up and in his turn
  Thus show'd his ready wit,
My head is twice as big as yours,
  They therefore needs must fit.

But let me scrape the dirt away
  That hangs upon your face;
And stop and eat, for well you may
  Be in a hungry case.

Said John—It is my wedding-day,
  And all the world would stare,
If wife should dine at Edmonton
  And I should dine at Ware.

So turning to his horse, he said,
  I am in haste to dine,
'Twas for your pleasure you came here,
  You shall go back for mine.

Ah, luckless speech, and bootless boast!
  For which he paid full dear;
For while he spake a braying ass
  Did sing most loud and clear.

Whereat his horse did snort as he
  Had heard a lion roar,
And gallop'd off with all his might
  As he had done before.

Away went Gilpin, and away
　　Went Gilpin's hat and wig;
He lost them sooner than at first,
　　For why? they were too big.

Now Mistress Gilpin, when she saw
　　Her husband posting down
Into the country far away,
　　She pull'd out half a crown;

And thus unto the youth she said
　　That drove them to the Bell,
This shall be yours when you bring back
　　My husband safe and well.

The youth did ride, and soon did meet
　　John coming back again,
Whom in a trice he tried to stop
　　By catching at his rein.

But not performing what he meant,
　　And gladly would have done,
The frighted steed he frighted more,
　　And made him faster run.

Away went Gilpin, and away
　　Went post-boy at his heels,
The post-boy's horse right glad to miss
　　The lumbering of the wheels.

Six gentlemen upon the road
  Thus seeing Gilpin fly,
With post-boy scampering in the rear,
  They raised the hue and cry.

Stop thief, stop thief—a highwayman!
  Not one of them was mute,
And all and each that pass'd that way
  Did join in the pursuit.

And now the turnpike gates again
  Flew open in short space,
The toll-men thinking as before
  That Gilpin rode a race.

And so he did, and won it too,
  For he got first to town,
Nor stopp'd till where he had got up
  He did again get down.

Now let us sing, Long Live the King,
  And Gilpin, long live he,
And when he next doth ride abroad,
  May I be there to see!

# "BRANES"

## Henry W. Shaw

"Branes are a sort ov animal pulp, and by common konsent are suppozed tew be the medium ov thought.

"How enny boddy knows that the branes do the thinking, or are the interpreters ov thought, iz more than i kan tell; and, for what i kno, this theory may be one ov thoze remarkable diskoverys ov man which ain't so.

"Theze subjeks are tew mutch for a man ov mi learning tew lift. i kant prove any ov them, and i hav too mucth venerashun tew guess at them.

"Branes are generally supozed tew be lokated in the hed, but investigashun satisfys me that they are planted all over the boddy.

"I find that a dansing master's are situated in hiz heels and toze, while a fiddler's all center in hiz elbows.

"Sum people's branes seem tew be placed in their hands and fingers, which explains their grate genius for taking things which they kan reach.

"I hav seen cases whare all the branes seemed

tew kongregate in the tongue; and once in a grate while they inhabit the ears, and then we hav a good listerner, but theze are seldum cases.

" Thare seeme tew be kases whare thare aint enny branes at all, but this iz a mistake. i thought i had cum akrost one ov theze kind once, but after watching the pashunt for an hour, and see him drink 5 horns ov poor whiskey during the time, i had no trouble in telling whare hiz branes all lay.

" I hav finally cum tew the konclushun that branes, or sum thing else that iz good tew think with, are excellent tew hav; but yu want tew keep yure eye on them, and not let them phool away their time, nor yures neither."

# EARLY RISING

## John Godfrey Saxe

"God bless the man who first invented sleep!"
 So Sancho Panza said, and so say I;
And bless him, also, that he didn't keep
 His great discovery to himself; nor try
To make it—as the lucky fellow might—
A close monopoly by patent right!


Yes—bless the man who first invented sleep
 (I really can't avoid the iteration);
But blast the man, with curses loud and deep,
 Whate'er the rascal's name, or age, or station,
Who first invented, and went round advertising,
That artificial cut-off—Early Rising!


"Rise with the lark, and with the lark to bed,"
 Observes some solemn, sentimental owl;
Maxims like these are very cheaply said;
 But, ere you make yourself a fool or fowl,
Pray just inquire about his rise and fall,
And whether larks have any bed at all!

The " time for honest folks to be a-bed "
   Is in the morning, if I reason right;
And he who cannot keep his precious head
   Upon his pillow till it's fairly light,
And so enjoy his forty morning winks,
Is up to knavery; or else—he drinks!

Thomson, who sung about the " Seasons " said
   It was a glorious thing to rise in season;
But then he said it—lying—in his bed
   At ten o'clock A. M.—the very reason
He wrote so charmingly. The simple fact is,
His teaching wasn't sanctioned by his practice.

'Tis, doubtless, well to be sometimes awake—
   Awake to duty, and awake to truth—
But when, alas! a nice review we take
   Of our best deeds and days, we find, in sooth,
The hours that leave the slightest cause to weep
Are those we passed in childhood or asleep!

'Tis beautiful to leave the world a while
   For the soft visions of the gentle night;
And free at last from mortal care and guile,
   To live, as only in the angel's sight,
In sleep's sweet realms so cosily shut in,
Where, at the worst, we only *dream* of sin!

So let us sleep, and give the Maker praise,
  I like the lad who, when his father thought
To clip his morning by hackneyed phrase
  Of vagrant worm by early songster caught,
Cried " Served him right!—It's not at all sur-
      prising;
The worm was punish'd, sir, for early rising! "

# CONTENTMENT

## Oliver Wendell Holmes

LITTLE I ask; my wants are few;
   I only wish a hut of stone
(A *very plain* brown stone would do)
    That I may call my own;
And close at hand is such a one,
In yonder street that fronts the sun.

Plain food is quite enough for me;
   Three courses are as good as ten;
If Nature can subsist on three,
    Thank Heaven for three.   Amen!
I always thought cold victual nice—
My *choice* would be vanilla-ice.

I care not much for gold or land;
   Give me a mortgage here and there,
Some good bank-stock, some note of hand,
    Or trifling railroad share—
I only ask that Fortune send
A *little* more than I shall spend.

Jewels are baubles; 'tis a sin
   To care for such unfruitful things;
One good-sized diamond in a pin,
    Some, *not so large,* in rings.
A ruby, and a pearl, or so,
Will do for me—I laugh at show.

My dame should dress in cheap attire
   (Good, heavy silks are never dear);
I own perhaps I *might* desire
    Some shawls of true Cashmere—
Some narrowy crapes of China Silk,
Like wrinkled skins on scalded milk.

I would not have the horse I drive
   So fast that folks must stop and stare;
An easy gait—two, forty-five—
    Suits me; I do not care;
Perhaps, for just a *single spurt,*
Some seconds less would do no hurt.

Of pictures, I should like to own
   Titians and Raphaels three or four—
I love so much their style and tone—
    One Turner, and no more,
(A landscape, foreground golden dirt),
The sunshine painted with a squirt.

Of books but few—some fifty score
  For daily use and bound for wear;
The rest upon an upper floor;
    Some *little* luxury *there*
Of red morocco's gilded gleam,
And vellum rich as country cream.

Busts, cameos, gems—such things as these,
  Which others often show for pride,
*I* value for their power to please,
    And selfish churls deride;
*One* Stradivarius, I confess,
*Two* Meerschaums, I would fain possess.

Wealth's wasteful tricks I will not learn,
  Nor ape the glittering upstart fool;
Shall not carved tables serve my turn,
    But *all* must be of buhl?
Give grasping pomp its double share—
I ask but *one* recumbent chair.

Thus humble let me live and die,
  Nor long for Midas' golden touch;
If Heaven more generous gifts deny,
    I shall not miss them *much*—
Too grateful for the blessing lent
Of simple tastes and mind content!

# AN ELEGY ON THE DEATH OF A MAD DOG

OLIVER GOLDSMITH

Good people all, of every sort,
  Give ear unto song;
And if you find it wondrous short
  It cannot hold you long.

In Islington there was a man
  Of whom the world might say
That still a goodly race he ran
  Whene'er he went to pray.

A kind and gentle heart he had,
  To comfort friends and foes;
The naked every day he clad,
  When he put on his clothes.

And in that town a dog was found,
  As many dogs there be,
Both mongrel, puppy, whelp, and hound,
  And curs of low degree.

This dog and man at first were friends,
   But when a pique began,
The dog, to gain his private ends,
   Went mad, and bit the man.

Around from all the neighboring streets,
   The wondering neighbors ran,
And swore the dog had lost his wits,
   To bite so good a man.

The wound it seemed both sore and sad
   To every Christian eye;
And while they swore the dog was mad,
   They swore the man would die.

But soon a wonder came to light,
   That showed the rogues they lied:
The man recovered of the bite,
   The dog it was that died.

# OLD GRIMES

## Albert Gorton Greene

Old Grimes is dead; that good old man
   We never shall see more:
He used to wear a long black coat,
   All button'd down before.

His heart was open as the day,
   His feelings all were true;
His hair was some inclined to gray—
   He wore it in a queue.

Whene'er he heard the voice of pain,
   His breast with pity burn'd;
The large, round head upon his cane
   From ivory was turn'd.

Kind words he ever had for all;
   He knew no base design:
His eyes were dark and rather small,
   His nose was aquiline.

He lived at peace with all mankind,
   In friendship he was true:
His coat had pocket-holes behind,
   His pantaloons were blue.

Unharm'd, the sin which earth pollutes
    He pass'd securely o'er,
And never wore a pair of boots
    For thirty years or more.

But good old Grimes is now at rest,
    Nor fears misfortune's frown:
He wore a double-breasted vest—
    The stripes ran up and down.

He modest merit sought to find,
    And pay it its desert:
He had no malice in his mind,
    No ruffles on his shirt.

His neighbors he did not abuse—
    Was sociable and gay:
He wore large buckles on his shoes,
    And changed them every day.

His knowledge, hid from public gaze,
    He did not bring to view,
Nor made a noise, town-meeting days,
    As many people do.

His worldly goods he never threw
    In trust to fortune's chances,
But lived (as all his brothers do)
    In easy circumstances.

Thus undisturb'd by anxious cares,
   His peaceful moments ran;
And everybody said he was
   A fine old gentleman.

# THE SANDAL-MAKER OF BABYLON

### WILL CARLETON

HE was rather a picturesque old man, upon a
prettily complex plan

With grim ability never hid to superintend what
others did,

And state—an effort's race being run—how
things that were done should have been done.

Nought e'er was made but he could tell how he
could have made it twice as well;

Nought e'er destroyed but he would bet that he
could have smashed it finer yet.

And this erratum of mankind sat, all day, a
moral and mental cat,

And threw the claws of his intellect at every
merit and defect,

And into the palace and the cot, and into what
men were and were not,

And into the deeds they struggled through and
into the things they failed to do,

Using the most uncalled-for cares with other people and their affairs,

And viewed with a supercilious smile the work
of the world; and made, meanwhile,

The poorest sandals under the sun—the sandal-
maker of Babylon.

No one was ever, since earth began, religious
    enough to please this man;
No one to the gods e'er bowed a knee that could
    have done it as low as he;
The tower of Belus, itself, he thought, if men had
    builded it as they ought,
Had been much pleasanter to the eye, and several
    hundred times as high;
He knew just how it came to pass, that Nebu-
    chadnezzar was fed with grass;
Could he have only had his way, the monarch's
    feed should have been of hay.
In fact, no person, high or low, had fault to con-
    ceal, or merit to show,
But he could figure it to a notch, and hold it up
    for the world to watch,
And yet, withal, his moral gait was that of a
    deep old reprobate,
Full of foolish actions shrewdly done—the san-
    dal-maker of Babylon.


No man was better able to tell how dead men
    might be living and well,
He knew the parts of the human frame, and every
    organ he called by name,
A theory of his own had he that man wasn't made
    as he ought to be;

Could have creation by him been done, the job
   would have been a better one.
No ill to mankind ever came but he had remedies
   for the same,
But never a word about them said until the suf-
   fering man was dead.
And yet, in spite of his mental wealth, he never
   had any kind of health;
The sickliest creature under the sun was the sandal-maker of Babylon.

You think to hear him talk, that he invented
   money itself.  He'd see
The gone-by chance of every trade—how every
   bargain should *have* been made.
He'd tell the rich why they were so; the poor,
   why they were not; could show
How even the king's great national purse might
   have been managed better or worse,
Yet had he one financial lack; he might be kicked
   to Susa and back,
And not a coin of any shape from his habiliments
   would escape;
Wealth always had contrived to shun the sandal-
   maker of Babylon.

But he began, unlucky elf, at criticizing the king
   himself;

And so his head, as one might say, endangered
    even itself one day;
For soon the king, with a humorous sense, re-
    quested of him an audience;
And said, " I have heard you cannot live beneath
    such government as I give;
There's no necessity for the same, and no one but
    ourselves to blame.
So, sage of the lapstone, do not grieve; I will
    give you every chance to leave;
This gallows you shall be hanged upon, O san-
    dal-maker of Babylon!"

The engine of death the old man scanned, and
    murmured, in accents soft and bland,
" Well, hang, if it does you any good; but I want
    it expressly understood
That were this gallows made by me, a deadlier
    weapon it would be.
I go to the other world, no doubt things over
    there need straightening out."

The monarch laughed, and lightly said, " You'd
    be a nuisance, alive or dead.
Go back to your stall and pound away, and think
    your thinkings and say your say."
" A foolish plan you have hit upon," said the san-
    dal-maker of Babylon.

And never again the old man stayed one happy
    day at his double trade.

" I do not like to retrain my head by anybody's
    permit," he said.

" If king were I and I were king, I wouldn't have
    spared him for anything."

And slow and surely, day by day, he lost his vigor
    and pined away.

They found him lying dead alone—sad sandal-
    maker of Babylon.


And even now throughout this earth (I tell the
    story for what 'tis worth)

They say his restless spirit runs, and makes its
    home with various ones.

Few families are so happy they have not a visit
    from him some day;

Few towns so blessed with fortune's smile that he
    doesn't live there for a while,

He will find fault till earth is done—crank san-
    dal-maker of Babylon.

# JEST 'FORE CHRISTMAS

### Eugene Field

Father calls me William, sister calls me Will,
Mother calls me Willie, but the fellers call me Bill!
Mighty glad I ain't a girl—ruther be a boy,
Without them sashes, curls an' things that's worn
    by Fauntleroy!
Love to chawk green apples an' go swimmin' in the
    lake—
Hate to take the castor-ile they give for bellyache!
'Most all the time, the whole year round, there ain't
    no flies on me.
But jest 'fore Christmas I'm as good as I kin be!

Got a yeller dog named Sport, sick him on the cat;
First thing she knows she doesn't know where she
    is at!
Got a clipper sled, an' when us kids go out to slide,
'Long comes the grocery cart, an' we all hook a ride!
But sometimes when the grocery man is worrited
    an' cross,
He reaches at us with his whip, an' larrups up his
    hoss,

An' then I laff an' holler, " Oh, ye never teched
  *me!* "
But jest 'fore Christmas I'm as good as I kin be!

Gran'ma says she hopes that when I git to be a
  man,
I'll be a missionarer like her oldest brother, Dan,
As was et up by the cannibuls that lives in Ceylon's
  Isle,
Where every prospeck pleases, an' only man is vile!
But Gran'ma she had never been to see a Wild
  West Show,
Nor read the life of Daniel Boone, or else I guess
  she'd know
That Buff'lo Bill an' cowboys is good enough for
  me!
*Excep'* jest 'fore Christmas, when I'm good as 1
  kin be.

And then old Sport he hangs around, so solemn-
  like an' still,
His eyes they seem a-sayin': " What's the matter,
  little Bill? "
The old cat sneaks down off her perch an' wonders
  what's become
Of them two enemies of hern that used to make
  things hum!

But I am so perlite an' tend so earnestly to biz,
That Mother says to Father: " How improved our
  Willie is!"
But Father, havin' been a boy hisself, suspicions me
When, jest 'fore Christmas, I'm as good as I kin
  be!


For Christmas, with its lots an' lots of candies,
  cakes, an' toys,
Was made, they say, for proper kids an' not for
  naughty boys;
So wash yer face an' bresh your hair, an' mind yer
  p's and q's,
An' don't bust out yer pantalooms, and don't wear
  out your shoes;
Say " Yessum " to the ladies and " Yessur " to the
  men,
An' when they's company, don't pass yer plate for
  pie again;
But, thinkin' of the things yer'd like to see upon
  that tree,
Jest 'fore Christmas be as good as yer kin be!

# A STRUGGLE FOR THE MASTERY

## EDWARD EGGLESTON

THE school had closed on Monday evening as
usual. The boys had been talking in knots all day.
Nothing but the bulldog in the slender, resolute
young master had kept down the rising storm. A
teacher who has lost moral support at home, cannot
long govern a school. Ralph had effectually lost his
popularity in the district, and the worst of it was
that he could not divine from just what quarter the
ill wind came, except that he felt sure of Small's
agency in it somewhere. Even Hannah had
slighted him, when he called at Means's on Monday morning to draw the pittance of pay that was
due him.

He had expected a petition for a holiday on
Christmas day. Such holidays are deducted from
the teacher's time, and it is customary for the boys
to "turn out" the teacher who refuses to grant
them, by barring him out of the schoolhouse on
Christmas and New Year's morning. Ralph had
intended to grant a holiday if it should be asked,
but it was not asked. Hank Banta was the ring-
leader in the disaffection, and he had managed to

283

draw the surly Bud, who was present this morning, into it. It is but fair to say that Bud was in favor of making a request before resorting to extreme measures, but he was overruled. He gave it as his solemn opinion that the master was mighty peart, and they would be beat anyhow, some way, but he would lick the master for two cents ef he warn't so slim that he'd feel like he was fighting a baby.

And all that day things looked black. Ralph's countenance was cold and hard as stone, and Shocky trembled where he sat. Betsey Short tittered rather more than usual. A riot or a murder would have seemed amusing to her.

School was dismissed, and Ralph, instead of returning to the Squire's, set out for the village of Clifty, a few miles away. No one knew what he went for, and some suggested that he had " sloped."

But Bud said he warn't that air kind. He was one of them air sort as died in their tracks, was Mr. Hartsook. They'd find him on the ground nex' morning, and he 'lowed the master war made of that air sort of stuff as would burn the dogon'd ole schoolhouse to ashes, or blow it into splinters, but what he'd beat. Howsumdever, he'd said he was a-goin' to help, and help he would; but all the sinno in Golier wouldn't be no account again the cute they was in the head of the master.

But Bud, discouraged as he was with the fear of Ralph's "cute," went like a martyr to the stake and took his place with the rest in the schoolhouse at nine o'clock at night. It may have been Ralph's intention to preoccupy the schoolhouse, for at ten o'clock Hank Banta was set shaking from head to foot at seeing a face that looked like the master's at the window. He waked up Bud and told him about it.

"Well, what are you a-tremblin' about, you coward?" growled Bud. "He won't shoot you; but he'll beat you at this game, I'll bet a hoss, and me, too, and make us both as 'shamed of ourselves as dogs with tin-kittles to their tails. You don't know the master, though he did duck you. But he'll larn you a good lesson this time, and me, too, like as not." And Bud soon snored again, but Hank shook with fear every time he looked at the blackness outside the windows. He was sure he heard footfalls. He would have given anything to be at home.

When morning came, the pupils began to gather early. A few boys who were likely to prove of service in the coming siege were admitted through the window, and then everything was made fast, and a " snack " was eaten.

" How do you 'low he'll get in? " said Hank, trying to hide his fear.

" How do I 'low? " said Bud. " I don't 'low nothin' about it. You might as well ax me where I 'low the nex' shootin'-star is a-goin' to drap. Mr. Hartsook's mighty onsartin. But he'll git in, though, and tan your hide fer you, you see ef he don't. *Ef* he don't blow up the schoolhouse with gunpowder! " This last was thrown in by way of alleviating the fears of the cowardly Hank, for whom Bud had a great contempt.

The time for school had almost come. The boys inside were demoralized by waiting. They began to hope that the master had " sloped." They dreaded to see him coming.

" I don't believe he'll come," said Hank, with a cold shiver. " It's past school-time."

" Yes, he will come, too," said Bud. " And he 'lows to come in here mighty quick. I don't know how. But he'll be a-standin' at that air desk when it's nine o'clock. I'll bet a thousand dollars on that. *Ef* he don't take it into his head to blow us up! " Hank was now white.

Some of the parents came along, accidentally of course, and stopped to see the fun, sure that Bud would thrash the master if he tried to break in. Small, on the way to see a patient, perhaps, reined up in front of the door. Still no Ralph. It was just five minutes before nine. A rumor now gained currency that he had been seen going to Clifty the evening before, and that he had not come back, though in fact Ralph had come back, and had slept at Squire Hawkins's.

"There's the master," cried Betsey Short, who stood out in the road shivering and giggling alternately. For Ralph at that moment emerged from the sugar-camp by the schoolhouse, carrying a board.

"Ho! ho!" laughed Hank, "he thinks he'll smoke us out. I guess he'll find us ready." The boys had let the fire burn down, and there was now nothing but hot hickory coals on the hearth.

"I tell you he'll come in. He didn't go to Clifty fer nothin'," said Bud, who sat still on one of the benches which leaned against the door. "I don't know how, but they's lots of ways of killin' a cat besides chokin' her with butter. He'll come in—*ef* he don't blow us all sky-high!"

Ralph's voice was now heard, demanding that the door be opened.

"Let's open her," said Hank, turning livid with fear at the firm, confident tone of the master.

Bud straightened himself up. "Hank, you're a coward. I've got a mind to kick you. You got me into this blamed mess, and now you want to craw-fish. You jest tech one of these 'ere fastenin's, and I'll lay you out flat on your back afore you can say Jack Robinson."

The teacher was climbing to the roof with the board in hand.

" That air won't win," laughed Pete Jones out-side. He saw that there was no smoke. Even Bud began to hope that Ralph would fail for once. The master was now on the ridgepole of the schoolhouse. He took a paper from his pocket, and deliberately poured the contents down the chimney.

Mr. Pete Jones shouted, " Gunpowder! " and set off down the road to be out of the way of the explosion. Dr. Small remembered, probably, that his patient might die while he sat here, and started on.

But Ralph emptied the paper, and laid the board over the chimney. What a row there was inside! The benches that were braced against the door were thrown down, and Hank Banta rushed out, rub-bing his eyes, coughing frantically, and sure that he had been blown up. All the rest followed, Bud bringing up the rear sulkily, but coughing and sneezing for dear life. Such a smell of sulphur as came from that schoolhouse!

Betsey had to lean against the fence to giggle.

As soon as all were out, Ralph threw the board off the chimney, leaped to the ground, entered the schoolhouse, and opened the windows. The school soon followed him, and all was still.

"Would he thrash?" This was the important question in Hank Banta's mind. And the rest looked for a battle with Bud.

"It is just nine o'clock," said Ralph, consulting his watch, "and I'm glad to see you all here promptly. I should have given you a holiday if you had asked me like gentlemen yesterday. On the whole, I think I shall give you a holiday, anyhow. The school is dismissed."

And Hank felt foolish.

And Bud secretly resolved to thrash Hank or the master, he didn't care which.

And Mirandy looked the love she could not utter.

And Betsey giggled.

# "LINCOLN'S OWN STORIES"

*Compiled by*
ANTHONY GROSS

" I WISH, Mr. President," said a government official after a disastrous defeat of the Union army, " that I might be a messenger of good news instead of bad. I wish I could tell you how to conquer or to get rid of those rebellious States."

At this President Lincoln looked up, and a smile came across his face as he said: " That reminds me of two boys out in Illinois who took a short cut across an orchard. When they were in the middle of the field they saw a vicious dog bounding toward them. One of the boys was sly enough to climb a tree, but the other ran around the tree, with the dog following. He kept running until, by making smaller circles than it was possible for his pursuer to make, he gained upon the dog sufficiently to grasp his tail. He held on to the tail with a desperate grip until nearly exhausted, when he called to the boy up the tree to come down and help.

" ' What for? ' said the boy.

" ' I want you to help me let this dog go.'

"Now," concluded the President, " if I could only let the rebel States go, it would be all right. But I am compelled to hold on to them and make them stay."

A woman once approached the President rather imperiously. " Mr. President," she said, very theatrically, " you must give me a colonel's commission for my son. Sir, I demand it, not as a favor, but as a right. Sir, my uncle was the only man that did not run away at Bladensburg. Sir, my father fought at New Orleans, and my husband was killed at Monterey."

" I guess, madam," answered Mr. Lincoln, dryly, " your family has done enough for the country. It is time to give somebody else a chance."

An officer had disobeyed, or failed to comprehend an order.

" I believe I'll sit down," said Secretary Stanton, " and give that man a piece of my mind."

" Do, do," said Lincoln; " write him now while you have it on your mind. Make it sharp. Cut him all up."

Stanton did not need a second invitation. It was a " bone-crusher " that he read to the President.

"That's right," said Lincoln; "that's a good one."

"Whom can I send it by?" mused the Secretary.

"Send it!" replied Lincoln, "send it! Why, don't send it at all. Tear it up. You have freed your mind on the subject, and that is all that is necessary. Tear it up. You never want to send such letters. I never do."

# WHY ANIMALS DO NOT LAUGH
## From Rabbit Roads

### By Dallas Lore Sharp

At one time my home was separated from the woods by only a clover-field. This clover-field was a favorite feeding ground for the rabbits of the vicinity. Here, in the early evening, they would gather to feed and frolic; and, not content with clover, they sometimes went into the garden for a dessert of growing corn and young cabbage.

Take a moonlight night in autumn and hide in the edge of these woods. There is to be a rabbit party in the clover-field. The grass has long been cut and the field is clean and shining; but still there is plenty to eat. The rabbits from both sides of the woods are coming. The full moon rises above the trees, and the cottontails start over. Now, of course, they use the paths which they cut so carefully the longest possible way round. They hop leisurely along, stopping now and then to nibble the sassafras bark or to get a bite of wintergreen, even quitting the path, here and there, for a berry or a bunch of sweet wood-grass.

" Stop a moment; this won't do! Here is a side-path where the briers have grown three inches since they were last cut off. This path must be cleared out at once," and the old buck falls to cutting. By the time he has finished the path a dozen rabbits have assembled in the clover-field. When he appears there is a *thump,* and all look up; some one runs to greet the newcomer; they touch whiskers and smell, then turn to their eating.

The feast is finished, and the games are on. Four or five rabbits have come together for a turn at hop-skip-and-jump. And such hop-skip-and-jump! They are professionals at this sport, every one of them. There is not a rabbit in the game that cannot leap five times higher than he can reach on his tiptoes, and hop a clean ten feet.

Over and over they go, bouncing and bouncing, snapping from their marvelous hind legs as if shot from a spring-trap. It is the greatest jumping exhibition that you will ever see. To have such legs as these is the next best thing to having wings.

Right in the thick of the fun sounds a sharp *thump! thump!* Every rabbit " freezes." It is the stamp of an old buck, the call, *Danger! danger!* He has heard a twig break in the woods, or has seen a soft, shadowy thing across the moon.

As motionless as stumps squat the rabbits, stiff with the tenseness of every ready muscle. They listen. But it was only a dropping nut or a restless bird; and the play continues.

They are chasing each other over the grass in a game of tag. There go two, round and round, tagging and retagging, first one being " it " and then the other. Their circle widens all the time and draws nearer to the woods. This time round they will touch the bush behind which we are watching. Here they come—there they go; they will leap the log yonder. Flash! squeak! scurry! Not a rabbit in the field! Yes; one rabbit—the limp, lifeless one hanging over the neck of that fox trotting off yonder in the shadows, along the border of the woods!

The picnic is over for this night, and it will be some time before the cottontails so far forget themselves as to play in this place again.

It is small wonder that animals do not laugh. They have so little play. The savage seldom laughs, for he hunts and is hunted like a wild animal, and is allowed so scant opportunity to be off guard that he cannot develop the power to laugh. Much more is this true of the animals. From the day an animal is born, instinct and training are bent toward the circumvention of enemies. There is no time to play, no chance, no cause for laughter.

The little brown rabbit has least reason of all to

be glad. He is utterly inoffensive, the enemy of none, but the victim of many. Before he knows his mother he understands the meaning of *Be ready! Watch!* He drinks these words in with his milk. The winds whisper them; the birds call them; every leaf, every twig, every shadow and sound, says: *Be ready! Watch!* Life is but a series of escapes, little else than vigilance and flight. He must sleep with eyes open, feed with ears up, move with muffled feet, and, at short stages, he must stop, rise on his long hind legs, and listen and look. If he ever forgets, if he pauses one moment for a word-less, noiseless game with his fellows, he dies. For safety's sake he lives alone; but even a rabbit has fits of sociability, and gives way at times to his feelings. The owl and the fox know this, and they watch the open glades and field edges. They must surprise him.

The barred owl is quick at dodging, but Bunny is quicker. It is the owl's soft, shadow-silent wings that are dreaded. They spirit him through the dusk like a huge moth, wavering and aimless, with dangling dragon-claws. But his drop is swift and certain, and the grip of those loosely hanging legs is the very grip of death. There is no terror like the ghost-terror of the owl.

The fox is feared; but then, he is on legs, not

wings, and there are telltale winds that fly before him, far ahead, whispering, *Fox, fox, fox!* The owl, remember, like the wind, has wings—wings that are faster than the wind's, and the latter cannot get ahead to tell of his coming. Reynard is cunning. Bunny is fore-sighted, wide-awake, and fleet of foot. Sometimes he is caught napping—so are we all; but if in wits he is not always Reynard's equal, in speed he holds his own very well with his enemy. Reynard is nimble, but give the little cottontail a few feet handicap in a race for life, and he stands a fair chance of escape, especially in the summer woods.

# EXTRACTS FROM LORD DUNDREARY AND HIS BROTHER SAM

## 1

### *Why the Family Settled in Britain*

It is the boast of many that their ancestors came over to Britain with the Conqueror. The illustrious family of Dundreary can claim a descent much more ancient. The first of the line who settled in Britain landed upon these shores nearly a thousand years before the Norman invasion. This distinguished personage, whose descent can be clearly traced back to Gomer, the eldest son of Japhet, became a Briton under very singular but interesting circumstances. He was a mere babe at the time when his father (a restless spirit of an inquiring mind, who had settled in Gaul) resolved to cross the sea to the white island, which he had often seen glimmering in the light of the setting sun as he impatiently paced the shores of Normandy. It is recorded in one of the chronicles that this progenitor of the family was very much in debt, and that his credit was failing in Gaul. We attach no belief whatever to this statement; but a narration in connection with it may be repeated as one of those pleasing myths with which history is so agreeably diversified.  Going one day into a place where wine was sold, Olog—that was his name—demanded a stoup of Burgundy, and requested the wineseller to affix a record of the transaction on a square slab of blue stone which hung on a nail behind the door. The wineseller protested that it was not in his power to effect the transaction in the manner indicated, and on being asked to explain himself said, as he withheld the flagon with his left hand:

" My Lord Olog, I have no chalk."

On hearing these awful words, the Lord Olog went away thirsting as he came, and wandered to the seashore.  And when he came to the seashore the sun was setting in the nor'west, casting his last slanting beams on the white cliffs of Albion.  And suddenly a brilliant thought—brilliant as the crimson gold which the dying sun bequeathed to the rippling waters—struck the Lord Olog.  And as it struck him, he stamped his foot and said:

" Yonder is the land of chalk—thither I go! "

And the Lord Olog took ship and sailed away with his only son, an infant, to Albion.

In order to guard against the extinction of his race by accident at sea—for Olog and his infant son were the last of the direct line—Olog engaged two ships, one for himself and one for his infant son. The two ships set sail together, but presently parted company and steered by different courses. A great storm arose immediately afterwards, and Olog's ship went down with Olog in it. The ship of the infant son resisted the fury of the waves, and after many days was run ashore at Brightelmstone, where the child was claimed as flotsam and jetsam by the Primate of the ancient order of the Druids.

## 2

### *The Saxon's Invitation to Britain*

In the reign of Vortigern, Dunderbert, descended in a direct line from Olog, occupied the post of Lord High Chamberlain, and had the honor of writing the letter to the Saxons inviting them to come over and settle in Britain. The art of writing was then in its infancy; and it will surprise no one who is acquainted with the first difficulties of the caligraphic art to hear that the writing of this epistle occupied Dunderbert three years, seven months and fourteen days. However, when the arduous task was completed, Dunderbert read the letter to the assembled court, and his manner of reading was so pleasing to the king and his courtiers that he was called upon to read it again. This he did, but with such increased effect that the king and the courtiers insisted upon a postscript, that they might have the pleasure of hearing **Dunder-bert** read still further.  On that occasion there were the loudest applause and shouts that were ever heard within the walls of a court.  The Saxons duly received the letter, and, after occupying five years, eleven months and twenty-nine days in deciphering it, joyfully responded to the invitation, and flocked to this country in such numbers that there was no room for them all, and many had to be turned away, though they offered money freely for admission. So great was the inroad that the king was obliged to issue a proclamation setting forth that no applications for admission to England, on the plea of privilege, could be attended to.  Thus did an ancestor of Lord Dundreary introduce the Saxons into Britain, and lay the foundations of that noble race which is now the glory of the world.

### 3

### *The Knight Under the Round Table*

Not to enter too minutely into the ancient history of the family, we may state generally and broadly that an ancestor of Lord Dundreary was one of King Arthur's knights; and it is related that on one occasion this knight was found—very late at night—*under* the Round Table. King Arthur, who loved a joke, left him where he was, and locked him into the upper chamber, where the feast was held. At the peep of day, however, the knight, who had dreamt that he was in the Dark Valley, awoke, and escaped from the window, letting himself down into the garden by the branch of the apple-tree just at the moment that the landlord of the hostel was about to slay a cat which had disturbed his rest during the night-watches by making a molrow on the tiles. The knight was just in time to save the life of the cat and punish the landlord. The affair made a great sensation in the neighborhood, and the king rewarded the knight by making him Master of the Horse and the Royal Mews.

4

*The Signing of the Magna Charta*

It is on record that a progenitor of his lordship was present at the signing of Magna Charta by King John; and, if history speak not falsely, but for this illustrious baron the charter of English liberty might never have been signed at all, and we should all, even at this day, be groaning under the yoke of tyranny and despotism. When the king took his seat in the middle of that field at Runny-mede, whither the barons had led him, he demanded at once the charter and pen and ink. The charter was immediately unrolled before the king.

" The pen and ink! " cried the king impatiently. " How shall I sign this detestable document without pen and ink? "

The barons looked at each other in consternation. They had brought the charter, but they had entirely forgotten the pen and ink.

" By my halidome! " said the king, " ye expect me to do impossibilities. Ye bring me here to sign, and there is not wherewithal to do it."

A baron of marvelous resource, who had meantime plucked a reed and cut it with his sword into the shape of a pen, here stepped forward and said—

" My liege, the pen."

" But the ink! " cried the king, more impatiently than before. " How can I sign without ink? "

The barons knew not what to do. Indeed they were so much at their wits' end that one of them suggested sending to Staines for ink, on the chance of finding it lying about somewhere, as the reed had just been found by the baron of marvelous resource. The king, who had justly become impatient, was on the point of rising to go, leaving the charter unsigned, when Roger le Toft (the illustrious ancestor of the present lord) stepped forward, and, presenting a small bottle, said:

" Your Majesty, the ink."

The king was so incensed that he could have knocked Le Toft's head off, notwithstanding that his hair was glossy and neatly parted down the back and middle; but he restrained himself, and ground his teeth with rage, while the barons around him stood amazed. Recovering themselves, however, they gave three cheers for Le Toft, and bade the king sign.

The king, with much reluctance, began his signature at one o'clock precisely, and had put the last flourish to the concluding X at twenty minutes past five, exclaiming as he did so:

" By my halidome, but this ink is faint!"

All the barons, as they signed their names, made the same remark, and reproached Le Toft for carrying such bad ink. But Le Toft nudged them and said, " Be thankful that ye have got any ink at all."

When the charter was signed and the king had gone, the barons openly made sport of Le Toft's ink.

" Now I do not fear to speak," said Le Toft. " It was not ink at all."

" Not ink!" cried all the barons in chorus. " In the name of St. George what was it then?"

" My private bottle of hair dye," said Le Toft, laughing.

This fully accounts for the exceeding faintness of the signatures to the document, which is still preserved in the British Museum.

## 5

### *The Earl in London*

On it being announced in the *Morning Post* that the youthful Earl of Dundreary had arrived in London for the season, the gilt knocker of the town mansion in St. James's Square was scarcely allowed to rest for a moment. His lordship was not only overwhelmed with visitors, but also with letters. Every new joint-stock company was desirous of receiving him as a director; every hospital and benevolent society solicited a donation and an annual subscription; every begging-letter writer appealed to his well-known generosity; while the tradesmen of the neighborhood clamored about the area steps of the noble mansion for the honour of his lordship's patronage.

Perplexed beyond measure by all these applications, the youthful lord summoned to his presence Buddicombe, his faithful valet.

" Buddicombe."

" Yes, my lord."

" Wat's all that wow and wingin at the bell down-stairs? "

" Butchers and bakers and milkmen, my lord, soliciting your lordship's patronage."

" How many are there of them? "

" Nearly a dozen, my lord, and I don't know which to choose."

" Well, it's a vewy difficult thing to know which baker and butcher to choose out of a dozen. If there were only one butcher and one baker, it—it would be compawatively eathy. What the dooth shall we do? Thtop, I have it. Thend them all up to me."

The faithful Buddicombe did as he was ordered; and there entered unto his lordship a whole brigade of commissariat officers, all most anxious to supply him with fish, flesh, and fowl.

Seeing a disposition among the purveyors to retire into corners, tread on each other's toes, and generally to get into confusion, his lordship addressed them in tones of command.

" Now then, my good people, I didn't thend for you to danthe a Scotch weel. Please to thtand in a wow. You want my cuthtom? "

The providers of fish, flesh, fowl, etc., nodded assent simultaneously.

" Vewy well," said his lordship.  " I'll tell you what I will do.  I will give you all a twial.  I'll twy you for a week each, and then if I like you, I'll give you all a turn, wegularly."

The purveyors grinned assent, each, of course, being confident that he would be the party selected for the honor of his lordship's permanent patronage.

" You like that awangement.  Vewy good; but there ith one condition.  I alwayth like to make conditions."

There was a chorus of " Yes, my lord."

" Oh,—on one condition, that you all supply me gwatis for the firtht week."

A blank and doubtful look here came over the faces of the purveyors.  His lordship appealed to Buddicombe.

" Eh—that'th fair; ithn't it, Buddicombe? "

" Yes, my lord, certainly," said Buddicombe.

" What do you thay to my pwoposition? " said his lordship.

The purveyors gave audible expression to murmurs and exchanged looks; but eventually a poulterer stood forward, and exhibiting an extended capon as a sample of his goods, respectfully accepted the terms.  A fishmonger, not to be outdone by the seller of fowls, immediately advanced, and holding out a turbot at arm's length, did like-wise.

" Vewy well; agweed! " said his lordship, and the purveyors retired one by one to go down-stairs in an ill-regulated manner, producing, by the aid of the milk-pails, a noise very closely resembling theatrical thunder.

" Buddicombe," said his lordship, " th-that was doothed clever. I never did anything tho tharp as that in my life."

" Very clever, your lordship."

" A-ha, a-ha! " laughed his lordship, in his peculiar manner. " E-hee, e-hee!—I'll get my wump chopth, and mutton thteaks and new-laid eggs fwesh from the cow for a week for nothing." [1]

" You are a great diplomatist, my lord," said Buddicombe.

" You think so, eh? "

" Certain of it, my lord."

" Well, y-eth, I think you're wight. I—I am a gweat diplo-diplomitht. I—I always knew I was a gweat diplo-ma-titht."

" Your lordship is evidently destined to make a figger in the Hupper 'Ouse of Parliament."

[1] Note by his Lordship: "I find I wathn't half tho clever as I thunk I was. The fellowth made me pay d-double for everything after the week wath out, ethpecially that fellow the fishmonger."—DUNDREARY.

" N-no, Buddicombe, you're wong there.  I—I never was good at making figures.  I—I used to get awful waps over the knuckles for my thwees and fi-hives.  I was vewy good at ones and elevens; but the cwooked ones were always a b-bother."

# THE BOOKWORM

Carolyn Wells

The Bookworm's an uninteresting grub,
Whether he's all alone or in a club.
Of stupid books which seem to us a bore,
A Bookworm will devour the very core.
Did Solomon or somebody affirm
The early reed-bird catches the book-worm?

# NOTES AND SUGGESTIONS

### THE OWL AND THE PUSSY-CAT
(Page 23)

The reader is asked to feel the poetic harmony and rhythm in this well-known nonsense song of Edward Lear. " Runcible " designates a spoon or fork having three broad tines.

### LAUGHING
(Page 25)

Josh Billings and Artemus Ward exhausted the possibility of fun in misspelling. Their stories make admirable silent reading, as the eyes will laugh at the distorted words.

### GOOD COUNSEL
(Page 27)

This selection is a nonsensical lesson in good manners, treated with serious " Good Counsel." The humor is founded on the assumption that inanimate objects possess human emotions, and are therefore sensible of our treatment.

### A PETITION OF THE LEFT HAND
(Page 29)

The humor of this selection is due to the sudden arrest of the reader's sympathy by the signature.

### No!
(Page 31)

In " No! " the pleasure comes from imitative harmony.

### THE EMPEROR'S NEW CLOTHES
(Page 33)

Here we have an example of humor due to illusion, or to unreality seemingly presented with ostentatious display.

### The Purple Cow
(Page 41)

The delicious absurdity of Mr. Burgess's rhyme has made it more often quoted than any other nonsense stanza.

### The Cataract of Lodore
(Page 42)

Lodore (Lō dōr') a cascade in Cumberland, England, near Keswick.

### Little Billee
(Page 48)

The fun in this poem is accentuated by sonorous adjectives, and by the incorrect use of pronouns.

Admiral Napier was Robert Cornelius Napier, made K. C. B. in recognition of his bravery at Lucknow.

### The Golden Reign of Wouter Van Twiller
(Page 50)

Apollo—in Greek, and later in Roman mythology, one of the great Olympian gods representing the light and life-giving influence. King Log—in Æsop's "Fables" a worthless and heavy log sent by Jove to the frogs who prayed for a King.

Note the Governor's substitute for legal papers (for a warrant and a summons).

Haroun-al-Raschid, Calif of Bagdad 786–809. He is best known from the tales of the "Arabian Nights," in which everything romantic and wonderful is connected with his name.

### A Christmas Eve Monologue
(Page 58)

This soliloquy may be used in a Christmas entertainment. It should be accompanied by dramatic action:— the effect will be enhanced by the entrance of "Pa" and "Ma" bearing a tree or a stocking filled with gifts, while the speaker is sleeping.

## The Owl-Critic
(Page 60)

Feel the approach of the joke; the effect of the refrain, " And the barber kept on shaving."

Audubon (John James) was a noted American ornithologist, who lived from 1780 to 1851 and spent many years in studying and drawing birds. His chief publication was " Birds of America."

John Burroughs was a noted American naturalist and writer. " Wake-Robin," " Signs," and " Seasons " are among his publications.

## Guido the Gimlet of Ghent: A Romance of Chivalry
(Page 64)

The ideal qualifications of a knight were courtesy, generosity, valor, and dexterity in arms.

Notice the effect gained by the use of archaic words:— " erstwhile "; the use of the prefix " be " in " begirt "; the resonant effect of the absurd title of the different knights and the entrance of the jester.

## The Wonderful " One-Hoss Shay "
(Page 75)

The reader should give himself up to the quiet merri-ment of Holmes' poems without too much analysis. The comic element in this poem expands as the cumulative virtues of the " Shay " give way, " Close by the meet'n-house on the hill."

## A Chapter from " Martin Chuzzlewit "
(Page 80)

Mark Tapley is Martin's servant and traveling companion. He is a light-hearted, merry fellow, who takes constant credit to himself for being jolly under the most adverse circumstances.

The comic spirit of Dickens deals with men and women in the lower walks of life.

### THE MAYOR OF SCUTTLETON
(Page 95)

This is a jingle that is purely foolish, and is included in this collection because of the absurdity from which it derives its charm. Others of a similar character are those on pages 57, 60, 182 and 204.

These rhymes should be read with the muscles of the face.

### THE ORIGIN OF ROAST PIG
(Page 96)

The humorous element in Lamb's stories is partially hidden by the seriousness of the argument.

### THE BIGELOW PAPERS
(Page 103)

*Gov'nor Seymour.* Horatio Seymour (1810–1886) New York, was one of the most prominent and respected men in the Democratic party, and a bitter opponent of Lincoln. He had at this time been recently elected Governor of New York on a platform that denounced almost every measure the government had found it necessary to adopt for the suppression of the Rebellion. . . .

" *Pres'dunt's Proclamation.*" In the autumn of 1862 Mr. Lincoln saw that he must either retreat or advance boldly against slavery. He had already proceeded far enough against it to rouse a dangerous hostility among Northern Democrats, and yet not far enough to injure the institution or enlist the sympathy of pronounced antislavery men. He determined on decisive action. On September 22, 1862, he issued a proclamation giving notice that on the first day of the next year he would, in the exercise of his war-power, emancipate all slaves of those States or parts of States in rebellion, unless certain conditions were complied with.

Mr. Lowell's fun comes from his masterly use of the Yankee dialect.

### FAITHLESS NELLY GRAY
(Page 112)

This punning ballad shows Hood's peculiar genius as a verbal humorist.

### THE WONDERFUL OLD MAN
(Page 115)

Our every-day habits of life are here presented so as to appear intensely funny.

### QUEEN ALICE
(Page 118)

Both matter and manner are amusing. An absurd situation is assumed and the consequences are detailed in simple seriousness. Lewis Carroll never lets his fancies become too funny, but he is always just funny enough.

The cleverness of the author's stories is not fully appreciated until they are dramatized.

### THE STRIKE
(Page 138)

Mr. Herford's poems are whimsical, yet they are more than humorous nonsense.

### THE TOWER OF LONDON
(Page 142)

In addition to his " grinning " words, Artemus Ward produces his humorous effects by assuming a manner of deep simplicity. His may be called the humor of simplicity.

The humor of the present day is worlds removed from the early American type. The merry god has learned that there is no necessity for twisting language into fantastic shapes in order to produce the comic.

### The Lobster Quadrille
(Page 147)

" The main interest of the vast majority of parodies is simply to amuse; but to amuse intelligently and cleverly. This aim is quite high enough."—*Carolyn Wells*.

This is a parody on the old story of The Spider and the Fly by Mary Howitt.

### Limericks
(Page 151)

Limerick (said to be from a custom at convivial parties according to which each member sang an extemporized " nonsense verse " which was followed by a chorus containing the words: " Will you come up to Limerick? ")

Mr. Lear has written 212 examples of this kind of verse.

### King Henry IV
(Page 152)

The humor of this extract is given in the words of Poins: " The virtue of jest will be, the incomprehensible lies that this same fat rogue will tell," etc.

Falstaff was said by William Hazlitt to be the most substantial comic character that ever was created.

Also the name of one of the thieves.

### Seein' Things
(Page 162)

The fun here comes largely from a " grown up " reading a " child's story."

### Old Chums
(Page 165)

This poem is an example of low and tender humor.

### WHY MR. DOG IS TAME
(Page 168)

In the delightful tales of Uncle Remus, we have as one source of merriment the ascription of human traits to animals. The charm of the negro dialect adds humor to the stories.

Every one should read " The Tar-Baby " by the same author.

### JENNY WREN
(Page 175)

The nourishing humor of Mother Goose's melodies " has survived whole generations and ages of pretenders to poetical inspiration."

One can scarcely read too much of this mild but adequate nonsense.

### MOTHER GOOSE RHYMES
(Page 181)

In reading these jingles, give yourself up entirely to the musical sound. Each bit of song forms an image of motion.

### SOLOMON GRUNDY
(Page 182)

These lines form an unmatchable biography, while Jenny Wren and Jack Sprat, Tommy Snooks and Bessie Brooks furnish clean-cut portraits.

### THE SUICIDAL CAT
(Page 198)

The superstition that a cat has nine lives is the thread of nonsense running through these rhyming lines.

### THE YONGHY-BONGHY-BO
(Page 204)

In this, as in many another of Lear's poems, we have words coined to suit the mellifluous sound of the rhymes.

### Condition and Way of Life of Don Quixote of La Mancha
#### (Page 209)

The main idea of Cervantes' story is to poke fun at the sentimental love for the order of chivalry. This idea is accomplished by making Don Quixote follow up his one idea to the exclusion of all else.

Watch for the interplay between the sublime and the ridiculous. Had Don Quixote himself known how to laugh, how much easier life would have been for him.

### Leedle Yawcob Strauss
#### (Page 219)

See the father's tender love peeping through the dialect of the poem.

### The Enchanted Shirt
#### (Page 221)

The office of humor here is to give to the king a picture of his own useless life.

### A Study in Piracy
#### (Page 225)

This " study " shows the humor of mimicry.

### A Tragic Story
#### (Page 249)

The paradoxical provokes the mirth in this poem.

### The Diverting History of John Gilpin
#### (Page 251)

The brisk movement of the poem adds to the comic portrait of Gilpin, although the laughable feature resides in the miserable situations in which Gilpin finds himself. Much humor is of this type—namely humor caused by seeing the hero in a " fix."

### EARLY RISING
(Page 264)

The comic element resides in the philosophic speculation over a commonplace custom.

### CONTENTMENT
(Page 267)

The author's affectation of sincere modesty is the cause of quiet laughter in " Contentment."

### AN ELEGY ON A MAD DOG
(Page 270)

Goldsmith's humor consists of a curious weaving together of that which amuses and that which touches the serious sentiments.

### OLD GRIMES
(Page 272)

Why do we laugh as we read this ballad? The reason is that each time that a virtue is mentioned, some physical characteristic obstinately obstructs our moral vision. In other words, the comic results when the body intrudes upon the soul.

### THE SANDAL-MAKER OF BABYLON
(Page 275)

The service of humor in this selection is that of self-correction by means of the laughable picture of the exaggeratedly important Sandal-maker.

### JEST 'FORE CHRISTMAS
(Page 280)

The obvious humor in these lines makes the poem a particularly good one for declamation.

### A STRUGGLE FOR THE MASTERY
(Page 283)

The schoolmaster furnishes an excellent example of the humor of surprise and suspense.

## " Lincoln's Own Stories "
### (Page 290)

The entire volume of " Stories " collected and edited by Anthony Gross is recommended to any reader interested in American humor.

## Lord Dundreary
### (Page 298)

Lord Dundreary is an indolent, foolish and amusing Englishman in Tom Taylor's comedy " Our American Cousin." E. A. Sothern, who played the part, has made the character famous.

# NOTES ABOUT AUTHORS

**Charles Follen Adams** (1842–1918) was an American writer of German dialect. Our selection, " Yawcob Strauss " is his most popular poem, yet one will find " Dot Long-Handled Dipper " and many of his other poems just as amusing.

**Hans Christian Andersen** (1850–1875) was a Danish writer. His fairy-tales are his best known works.

**Charles Farrar Browne,** Pseudonym Artemus **Ward,** (1834–1867) takes front rank for spontaneous native humor. His chief work is " Artemus Ward: His Book." He also wrote " Artemus Ward: His Travels," etc.

**(Frank) Gelett Burgess** is an author and grotesque draughtsman. He contributes to various American and English periodicals. " The Burgess Nonsense Book " is one of his many nonsense books.

**Will Carleton** (1845–1912) was the author of several volumes of poems chiefly illustrative of American rural life. His poems are often in dialect. " Farm Ballads " is one of Mr. Carleton's entertaining books.

**Alice Cary** (1820–1871) was an American author. Her writings include poems, novels, and sketches of Western life. " Her works bear the true stamp of genius— simple, natural and truthful—they evince a keen sense of the humor and pathos of the comedy and tragedy of life in the country."

**Miguel de Cervantes** (1547–1616) was a Spanish poet and novelist. His chief work is " Don Quixote," translations of which have appeared in every European language including Turkish. An English critic has said of this romance, " It is to Spain what Shakespeare is to England —the one book to which allusions may be made without affectation, but not missed without discredit."

**William Cowper** (1731–1800) was a celebrated English poet. He published translations of Homer's Iliad and Odyssey; was a writer of prose as well as poetry. " John Gilpin " is undoubtedly his most humorous poem.

**Josephine Dodge Daskam** contributes poems and stories to magazines. Among her writings are: " The Biography of a Boy," " Memoirs of a Baby," " While Caroline Was Growing." Our selection " A Study in Piracy " is taken from " The Madness of Philip." We recommend the other stories contained in this book to all boys and girls who are fond of laughter fused with kindliness.

**Charles Dickens** (1812–1870) was a celebrated English novelist usually grouped with Thackeray. Dickens portrayed the lower classes of society while Thackeray wrote of the upper classes. The author urges all boys and girls to become acquainted with the characters which Dickens portrays by vivid word pictures in " David Copperfield," " Nicholas Nickleby," " Oliver Twist," and other of his books.

**Mary Mapes Dodge** (1838–1905) was an American authoress, and for many years editor of St. Nicholas. One of her best books is " Hans Brinker."

**Charles Lutwidge Dodgson**, Pseudonym Lewis Carroll (1832–1898) was an English clergyman, writer, and mathematical lecturer at Christ Church, Oxford. He has written several children's books among which " Alice in Wonderland " is his best known.  Our selection is taken from " Through the Looking-Glass."

" The sweet figure of little Alice contrasts delightfully all through the book with the funny creatures and people she meets in her most exciting journey, and as she never makes a slip in her manners or loses her sense of propriety in the most trying situations, her story may be considered as strictly moral as it is exquisitely humorous."

**William H. Drummond** (1854–1907) deals with the French-Canadian character in his dialect poetry.  Numbered among his best poems are: " How Bateese Came Home," " Le Vieux Temps," " The Wreck of the *Julie Plante.*"

**Edward Eggleston** (1837–1902) was an American author.  Among his chief works of fiction are the " Hoosier Schoolboy " and the " Hoosier Schoolmaster."  He has also written a " History of the United States," and other well-known books.

**Eugene Field** (1850–1895) was an American journalist and poet.  His poems show a rare combination of humor and pathos.  Among his writings are: " Love Songs for Children," " Lullaby Land."

**James Thomas Fields** (1817–1881) was an American publisher and author.

**Benjamin Franklin** (1706–1790) was a celebrated American philosopher, statesman, diplomat, and author.  All American school children should read his " Autobiography " and become acquainted with the charming stories connected with Franklin's life.

**Oliver Goldsmith** (1728–1774) was a noted English poet, novelist, and dramatist.  His best known poem is

" The Deserted Village " and one of his best stories is
" The Vicar of Wakefield."

**Albert Gorton Greene** (1802–1868).  " The pathos,
quaint humor and abounding charity of ' Old Grimes '
presents a perfect picture of the moral qualities of its
author." The monody was written for a college society at
the age of sixteen.

**Joel Chandler Harris** (1848–1908) was an American
writer and journalist.  He is best known as the author of
books on negro folk-lore: " Uncle Remus: His Songs and
His Sayings," " Nights with Uncle Remus," " Mr. Rabbit
at Home," etc.

**John Hay** (1838–1905) was an American author, journalist, and diplomat.  From 1861–1865 he was assistant
private secretary to President Lincoln.

**Oliver Herford** is a writer of humorous fables and verse.
A great part of Mr. Herford's works belongs to the realm
of pure fancy.  His book, " The Bashful Earthquake, and
Other Fables and Verses " will amuse all boys and girls.

**Oliver Wendell Holmes** (1809–1894) the poet and wit
of Boston, was also a noted physician, professor and prose
writer.  He was the author of a series of delightful books,
beginning with the " Autocrat of the Breakfast-Table "
and ending with " Over the Teacups." Some of our best
humorous and patriotic poems were written by Dr. Holmes.

**Thomas Hood** (1798–1845) was an English poet and
humorist who took his place in the front rank of the funny
men of his time.  " The Song of the Shirt " is his most
popular poem.  " Like every author distinguished for true
comic humor, there was a deep vein of melancholy pathos
running through his mirth."

**Washington Irving** (1783–1859) was almost the first American author who gained a wide reputation. His humorous history of New York is one of his best works. Rip Van Winkle, the Legend of Sleepy Hollow and other interesting stories may be found in " The Sketch Book."

**Charles Lamb** (1775–1834) was a noted English man of letters, critic and humorist. " His wit is unwearied and his gentleness of heart ever uppermost, save when he chooses to be sarcastic; and then he soothes whomever he offends by some happy and unhoped-for compliment." Together he and his sister Mary wrote " Tales from Shakespeare."

**Stephen Butler Leacock,** Head of the Department of Political Economy in McGill University, Montreal, has published " Nonsense Novels," " Sunshine Sketches of a Little Town," and a great number of articles and sketches for amusement in hours of leisure.

**Edward Lear** (1812–1888) was an English artist and writer. Mr. Lear, like Lewis Carroll, was a deep thinker and a hard worker. Yet he is best known for his " Books of Nonsense," which are a real contribution to the pleasure of nations. Many of his nonsense songs have been set to music by talented composers.

**Abraham Lincoln** (1809–1865). Our readers will need no biography of the martyred president. The three of his stories that are to be found in this volume are taken from " Lincoln's Own Stories " by Anthony Gross. Mr. Lincoln did not tell his stories for the purpose of making conspicuous his sense of humor. He called into being his stories, as our examples show, to serve some purpose, or to illuminate some argument.

**James Russell Lowell** (1819–1891). Lowell, Longfellow, Bryant, Whittier, and Holmes belong to the group known as the New England poets. Lowell was a great critic as well as a great poet. During the Mexican and the Civil Wars he wrote a series of poems called " The Bigelow Papers." These gave a humorous view of American politics.

**Mother Goose** is a name famous in nursery literature through the familiar jingles called " Mother Goose Melodies."

**Frederick Moxon.** His writings may be found in the leading magazines and periodicals of the day.

**James Whitcomb Riley** (1853–1916) was a poet and public reader. He was for some years a painter, and later a journalist. He wrote a great many dialect poems and unusually charming poems of childhood and nature.

**John Godfrey Saxe** (1816–1887) was an American poet, journalist, and lecturer. He is best known for his humorous poems.

**William Shakespeare** (1564–1616) was a famous English poet, the greatest of dramatists. He was an actor as well as a writer of comedies, tragedies, and historic plays. Many of his stories were frankly taken from other writers, but the beauty and power of his plays are all his own. A great critic said of him: " Never was there such a wide talent for the drawing of character as Shakespeare's." Among his greatest plays are " Hamlet," " Macbeth," " Julius Cæsar," " Romeo and Juliet," " Midsummer Night's Dream," and " As You Like It."

**Henry Wheeler Shaw** (1818–1885), pseudonyms " Josh Billings " and " Uncle Esek," was an American humorist. He was a lecturer and published annually " Josh

Billings' Farmers' Allminax." His complete works were published in 1877.

**Dallas Lore Sharp** was born on a farm in Haleyville, N. J.

Love of nature and sympathy with wild life is the dominant characteristic of Mr. Sharp's books, yet there is much genuine humor woven into his studies of life out-of-doors.

One should read all the stories in " A Watcher in the Woods."

**Robert Southey** (1774–1843) was an English poet and prose-writer. He was made poet laureate in 1813.

**William Makepeace Thackeray** (1811–1863) was one of the greatest of English novelists. Among his great novels are " Pendennis," " The Newcomes," " Vanity Fair," and " Henry Esmond." An American critic who was once asked which of these he liked best replied: " The one I read last." Thackeray also wrote verse. Every one should become acquainted with the characters which Thackeray draws from the upper classes of society.

**John Townsend Trowbridge** (1827–1916) was an American novelist, poet, and editor. Among his best-known works are " Cudjo's Cave," " The Drummer Boy," " The Three Scouts," " Neighbor Jackwood," and " The Silver Medal Stories." His best-known poem next to " Darius Green and His Flying-Machine " is " The Vagabond."

**Carolyn Wells** has been engaged in literary work since 1895. She is the author of many books, and contributes articles, chiefly of a humorous nature, to current periodicals.